VOCABULARY BUILDER 2

BERNARD SEAL

Longman

Addison Wesley Longman Limited,
Edinburgh Gate, Harlow,
Essex CM20 2JE, England
and Associated Companies throughout the world.

First published 1988
Eleventh impression 1996

British Library Cataloguing in Publication Data
Seal, Bernard
    Vocabulary Builder.
    2
    1. English language. Vocabulary-
    Questions & answers-For non-English
    speaking students
    I. Title
    428.1'076

    ISBN 0-582-96501-2

Set in 9/10 Helvetica 765
Printed in China
SWTC/11

Illustrated by Michael Charlton, Joseph McEwan,
Gillian Martin, David Parkins, Liz Roberts and
Pat Tourret

Contents

Introduction

To the student

This book is intended to help you expand your vocabulary. It is written for students who are approaching the intermediate level. While studying *Vocabulary Builder 2*, it is a good idea for you to use a dictionary for intermediate learners of English, such as the *Longman Active Study Dictionary*.

Vocabulary Builder 2 is divided into three sections: **At home, At play** and **At work**. Each section has ten units that deal with different groups of words, and each unit contains several parts.

The first part is called **Words in context** and contains a passage or passages for you to read and study. You should try to read these passages without a dictionary. The key words are in dark print and in most cases you should be able to guess the meanings of these words from the way they are used in the passage. If you are not sure of the meaning of a word, always look back at the sentence before and after it. These sentences will often help to explain the word. You should also have a general idea of the meaning, because all the key words are closely related. For example, the first unit is called **Parts of the house** and all the key words (kitchen, fence, stairs, hall, basement, etc.) are all connected in some way to houses. This should help you guess the meanings of any words that you don't know.

Exercise 1 follows the **Words in context** passage. This is a reading comprehension exercise. In many cases the questions focus on the meanings of the key words.

Exercise 2 and **Exercise 3** test your knowledge of the key words in the passage. Before you do these exercises you should always look back at the passage and see how the key words have been used.

Each unit also has a fourth exercise called either **Dictionary work** or **Just for fun**. The **Dictionary work** exercise introduces more vocabulary related to the subject of the unit. You will usually need a dictionary for this exercise because you do not have a passage to help you guess the meaning of the words. The **Just for fun** exercises give you a chance to have some fun with the words you have been studying. For some of these exercises, it will be helpful if you can talk to someone who is also studying English so that you can share your ideas.

The final section, **Think about**, is also best done with a friend. It should help you to use the words in an interesting discussion.

You can study the units in any order you like, but it is best to study them in groups of five, e.g. units 1.1–1.5 or 2.6–2.10. Then, at the end of each five units, you can review the words you have studied in the **Vocabulary review** section. You can then also test your knowledge of these words in one of the six **Test yourself** exercises.

There is also an **Index** of key words at the back of the book which includes a phonetic guide to pronunciation. The **Index** gives the number of each unit in which the word appears.

To the teacher

Vocabulary Builders can be used either as classroom material or as self-study material for pre-intermediate to intermediate students who want to build their vocabulary.

The approach

Vocabulary Builders present key words in lexical sets embedded in texts. The meanings of the items can often be guessed from their context, and knowledge of the words is extended, practised and tested in a series of exercises.

Each book is divided into three large subject areas, containing ten units. Each unit teaches a lexical set, such as different housecleaning chores, adjectives used in describing food, types of television programmes, or ways of describing your health. There are two principal reasons for teaching vocabulary in sets. First, students often feel that they learn vocabulary in a somewhat random way. Putting the words into lexical sets makes their study more structured. Each unit studied then gives a sense of measurable progress. Secondly, since all the words in a lexical set are related, the student has an immediate clue as to the meaning of a previously unknown word. Thus, for example, when encountering the word 'shoot' in the unit 'Actions in sports' the student will realize that it is something that a sportsperson does while playing a sport.

Each lexical set is presented in a reading passage or passages at the beginning of a unit. These passages may seem difficult. The syntax and structures in them have not been tightly controlled and you may well feel that the language is beyond the productive capabilities of your students. This has been done intentionally. The aim is to have students reading at a level that stretches and challenges them, provided that they are able to maintain a general sense of what the text is about.

The passages have been carefully written so that the more difficult lexical items can be guessed from the context in which they occur. This may often involve a certain degree of textual redundancy which enables the meaning of the target items to be made clearer by the extra clues. Given these clues, the students learn to guess the meanings of words from their contexts and are encouraged not to become too dependent on the dictionary while they are reading. It is important that students develop good reading habits. They should learn to read fluently, tolerating a certain degree of ambiguity while maintaining an interest in the gist of the passage.

The target words are clearly marked in a bold typeface on their first occurrence in the text. Each target item occurs again in at least one of the exercises that follow. These exercises are designed to reinforce the meanings of the target words and to test the students' understanding of how they should be used. The fact that each target item appears in bold print enables the students to return to the original **Words in context** passage to find an example of its usage. This will help them do the exercises.

Contents of a unit

● *Words in context*
A short passage or passages containing the target words in the lexical set.

- *Exercise 1*

A comprehension exercise which leads students to understand the overall meaning of the passage and at the same time focuses attention on some of the key vocabulary items.

- *Exercises 2 and 3*

Each of the target lexical items is encountered in at least one of these exercises. The exercises are designed to extend the students' understanding of the items.

- *Dictionary work/Just for fun*

Dictionary work exercises encourage students to expand their vocabulary by introducing a lexical set related to the topic of the unit. The students will usually need a dictionary to complete these exercises.

Just for fun exercises may take various forms: ranking and rating exercises, games, and other communicative activities. These exercises are intended to further the students' interest in the topic and to give them an opportunity to use some of the target lexical items in a stress-free context.

- *Think about*

These are discussion questions, designed to activate the students' production of the target words in a conversation or discussion.

How to use Vocabulary Builders in the classroom

Each unit is designed so that it can form the basis for a one-hour lesson. However, the material should be flexible enough to be used in parts over a series of lessons if preferred. Teachers may also find that they can use the book to combine in-class work with self-study.

One of the main aims of the *Vocabulary Builders* is to promote a problem-solving approach to vocabulary learning. On their first encounter with the target items in the reading passages, students are expected to try to work out the meanings without much teacher guidance and without the use of a dictionary. Be aware, therefore, that too much pre-teaching will destroy the point of the exercises. It is suggested that you introduce the topic of the unit with some brief pre-questions relating to the topic. Then, if you want to pre-teach some vocabulary items, only pre-teach those words that you feel will facilitate your students' understanding of the text, but which are not key words i.e. words which do not appear in bold print in the text.

The first time you use the book, you should explain to the students why you do not want them to use a dictionary when studying the passages. Point out how many of the difficult words can be guessed from their context. This may be illustrated by taking one of the passages and going through it with the class. The students will soon get used to searching for the context clues and doing without a dictionary.

Let your students work silently once they start reading the passage. When they are ready they should attempt to answer the questions in **Exercise 1**. Encourage students to share their answers in pairs.

At this stage (when all the students have read the passage and attempted **Exercise 1**) you may want to read the passage aloud so they can hear how the words are pronounced. Your phrasing may also help the students to understand the passage better. It is best if you wait until they have read through the passage silently before they hear it, because this promotes the habit of silent reading when they are on their own.

Exercise 2 and **Exercise 3** may then be done either as whole class or pair work activities or individually, whichever seems more appropriate. In general, easier exercises should be done individually, with the students checking their answers with their neighbours, and more difficult problem-solving exercises should be done in pairs or small groups.

Just for fun exercises are designed for work in pairs or small groups. Make sure the students are absolutely clear about what they have to do in their groups. This should be a relaxed, active and enjoyable phase of the lesson.

Dictionary work exercises may either be done in class with dictionaries or set as homework.

The **Think about** questions are intended to get students talking and using the vocabulary of the lesson. There are only a few discussion questions in each unit so you may wish to add some of your own.

There are twenty-five test sentences in each **Test yourself** section: five for each of the previous five units. Having completed one unit, you may, therefore, want to set your students the task of finding and answering the five sentences in the **Test yourself** section that test the use of five of the key words in that unit. Alternatively, to make most effective use of the **Test yourself** sections, teach the units in groups of five, i.e. units 1.1 to 1.5 or 2.6 to 2.10. Then set your students the **Test yourself** section.

It is possible to teach the units in any order. They have not been sequenced in difficulty and do not rely on the students having studied one unit in order to study the next.

Acknowledgements

To those who use this book it may seem as though such a small and simple book could not have required too much pain and effort. Be undeceived. Many hours of work, many revisions, much testing and a great deal of discussion have gone into the creation of these few pages.

Many people at Longman have made substantial contributions, in particular, Malcolm Booker, Susan Maingay, Della Summers and Deborah Tricker. As usual, the English Language Centre in Hove, Sussex, has provided me with essential facilities. Special thanks to Dr Ian Dunlop, Norma Williams and Dave Brown, Colleagues, too, at the American Language Institute at the University of Southern California have helped by testing materials and giving much needed moral support. Thanks, also, are due to Robert O'Neill for valuable input in the developmental stages of the project.

Finally, let me acknowledge the contribution of my wife, Chris, who, being an ESL teacher herself, has not only helped with ideas, tested materials, and suggested changes, but has also had to fortify me during some of the more frustrating moments of getting the book completed.

1 At home

1.1 Parts of the house

Words in context

Read the following passage and do the exercises.

Mr Hudson sells houses. At the moment he is showing 736 Pearblossom Avenue to Mr and Mrs Willis.

'Here we are. As you can see, Mr and Mrs Willis, it's really quite a big house, with two **storeys**. **Upstairs** there are three **bedrooms** and a **bathroom**, and **downstairs** we have a large **living room**, a **dining room**, and a **kitchen**. There is no **basement** under the house.

'Before we go in, let's take a look at the house from the outside. I think you'll agree that the **front garden** is a nice size and the **hedge** around it makes it a little more private. You've got a car, haven't you? So the **garage** next to the house will be very useful. Now, look up there at the **roof**. It was repaired only four months ago, so you won't have any trouble from the rain. The **chimney** up there doesn't work any more. You see, the **fireplaces** were taken out when the **central heating** was put in.

'O.K. Let's go in here through the garden **gate** and up the **path** to the **front door**. Follow me.

'I'll just open the door and here we are inside. Here's a little **hall** where you can hang your hats and coats. On your right is the living room, and this door on your left leads into a small dining room. As you can see, it has a lovely wooden **floor**. The dining room and the kitchen are connected, so you can cook in the kitchen and serve the meals in the dining room. From the kitchen **window** you have a pleasant view of the **back garden**, which, as you can see, has a strong wooden **fence** around it.

'The house is in excellent condition. You'll have no problems with any of the **walls**, floors or **ceilings**. So, any questions? Ah, yes, the price. Three bedrooms, a garage and a garden. Well, what do you think?'

Exercise 1

Label the parts of the house with the letters from the list on the left.

a) the kitchen

b) the back garden

c) the hall

d) the living room

e) the front garden

f) the garage

g) the dining room

h) the stairs

i) the front door

j) the path

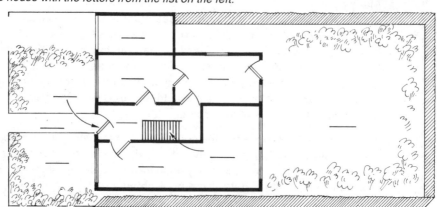

Exercise 2

What are these rooms used for? Match each part of the house with what usually happens in it.

1 _____ the kitchen		a) a place to wash
2 _____ the dining room		b) a place to sleep
3 _____ the bedroom		c) a place to hang coats
4 _____ the garage		d) a place to relax and talk
5 _____ the garden		e) a place to cook
6 _____ the bathroom		f) a place to grow flowers
7 _____ the living room		g) a place to keep a car
8 _____ the hall		h) a place to eat

Exercise 3

Which part of the house is different from the other three in each group?

1	a) floor	b) wall	c) stairs	d) ceiling
2	a) fireplace	b) roof	c) central heating	d) chimney
3	a) bathroom	b) garage	c) kitchen	d) bedroom
4	a) window	b) wall	c) gate	d) door
5	a) downstairs	b) upstairs	c) basement	d) storey
6	a) fence	b) path	c) hedge	d) wall

Just for fun

Which would you most like to have in a house? Put the following in order from most important (1) to least important (6). Then discuss your answers with someone else.

a large bedroom	_____	a large comfortable living room _____
a large modern kitchen _____		a large bathroom _____
a large garden	_____	a garage _____

Think about

1 Think of a house you know and describe it to a friend. Then ask them to draw a plan of the house.
2 How much does the average house cost in your country? What makes one house more expensive than another?
3 Describe a very traditional type of house in your country.

1.2 Furniture and furnishings

Words in context *Read the following dialogue and do the exercises.*

It is the twenty-fifth century. A group of schoolchildren is visiting the National Museum of the Past. One child has a lot of questions for the tour guide.

GUIDE: We are now entering a typical living room of the late twentieth century.

CHILD: What's that box in the middle of the room? It seems as if all the **chairs** are placed so that people could sit and look at it.

GUIDE: That's right. That box is called a **television set**. People used to look at the pictures on it for hours and hours. They used to sit in those **armchairs** or on the **sofa**, which is that big chair for two or three people.

CHILD: Did people have machines for listening to music in those days, like we do now?

GUIDE: Yes, of course. This machine in the corner is called a **stereo system**. It has three parts. This part on top was used for playing round black disks called **records**. Underneath that, you can see the **radio**. And underneath the radio, there's a **cassette recorder**, which was used for playing music on tape.

CHILD: What's that low **table** in front of the sofa? Is that a kind of **desk**?

GUIDE: No, their desks were much bigger, and they had **drawers**. That's called a **coffee table**. In those days people used to drink something called coffee and smoke things called cigarettes. They used to put their coffee cups on this table while they were watching television. They dropped the ash from their cigarettes into that glass dish. That's why it's called an **ashtray**. Coffee and cigarettes have been illegal for the last two hundred and fifty years.

CHILD: And what are those things on the **shelves** over there behind the **dining table**? Are they books?

GUIDE: Yes, they are. And the piece of furniture with the shelves is called a **bookcase**.

CHILD: Didn't they have **computers**?

GUIDE: Yes, they did. Personal computers were invented towards the end of the century and revolutionized everyone's lives. Now then, I'd like someone to turn off that old **lamp** by pressing the **switch** on its side. I'll draw the **curtains** to make the room a bit darker and we'll turn on this television and watch a very popular twentieth-century film for children. It's about a mouse called Mickey.

Exercise 1

Circle those things which probably do not exist in the twenty-fifth century, according to the conversation between the guide and the child.

1 books	6 lamps	11 shelves
2 coffee	7 records	12 machines for playing music
3 televisions	8 radios	13 cigarettes
4 chairs	9 computers	14 dining tables
5 desks	10 sofas	15 Mickey Mouse films

Exercise 2

Match the words with the pictures.

| a) armchair | b) dining table | c) lamp | d) switch | e) bookcase | f) desk | g) sofa | h) drawer |

1 _____   2 _____   3 _____   4 _____

5 _____   6 _____   7 _____   8 _____

Exercise 3

Complete the sentences using the words below.

| ashtray | window | stereo system | cassette recorder | coffee table | shelf |

1 Put the book on the _____.

2 Put the record on the _____.

3 Put the cup on the _____.

4 Put out your cigarette in the _____.

5 Put the tape in the _____.

6 Draw the curtain across the _____.

Dictionary work

Put the following items into the correct columns. Do as many as you can and then check your answers in a dictionary.

| a deckchair | a cupboard | a wardrobe | a stool | a carpet | a cabinet |
| a bench | a chest of drawers | a rug | a mat | a cushion | linoleum |

to sit on	**to put things in**	**to walk on**
_____	_____	_____
_____	_____	_____
_____	_____	_____
_____	_____	_____

Think about

1 What furniture do you have in your living room?

2 What furniture do you usually find in the different rooms of a house in your country?

3 Do you have a television, a stereo system, a telephone? If you could have only one of these things, which would you choose?

1.3 Sleeping

Words in context *Read the following passage and do the exercises.*

It's late. You're **tired**. It's been a long day and you're ready to **go to bed**. You're feeling **sleepy**. You can hardly keep your eyes open. So you take your clothes off, put on your **pyjamas**, brush your teeth, wash your hands and face, and get ready to get into bed. You pull back the **blankets**, get in between the **sheets** and rest your head on the **pillow**.

The **mattress** under you feels just right, not too hard and not too soft. Maybe you start reading a book, but you're **exhausted**, and in a few minutes your eyes get heavy. You can't stay **awake** any longer. You start to get **drowsy**. You turn the light out and soon, very soon, you begin to **fall asleep**. You are half asleep already. And then quite suddenly you move from **consciousness** to **unconsciousness** and you are asleep.

(Now answer question 1, Exercise 1.)

But then what happens?

In the first hour of a normal night's sleep, you go into a **deep sleep**. In fact, this is the time when your sleep is deepest. Then, later in the night, the mind goes into a lighter sleep, called by scientists 'paradoxical sleep'. It is during this type of sleep that you have your **dreams** (or **nightmares**!). In a normal night, most people go from deep sleep to paradoxical sleep about four or five times. Each period of deep sleep becomes less deep and shorter, and each period of paradoxical sleep becomes longer and lighter. Finally you have your last period of paradoxical sleep and your last dream. Then you **wake up**. And now that you are awake, it's time to **get up**.

(Now answer question 2.)

Exercise 1

1 *Name the things in the pictures.*

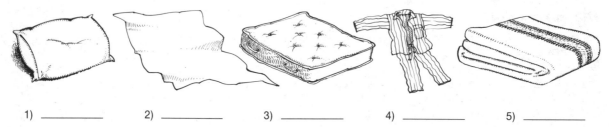

1) _____   2) _____   3) _____   4) _____   5) _____

2 *Look at these diagrams. Which one shows a normal night's sleep?*

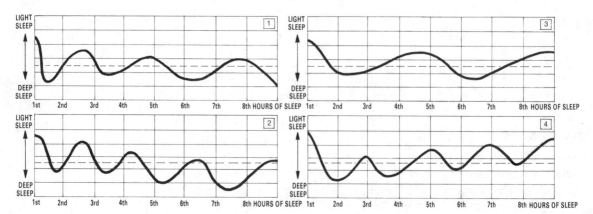

Exercise 2

Match each word or phrase on the left with a word or phrase of similar meaning on the right.

1 _____ in a conscious state   a) get out of bed

2 _____ bad dream   b) lie down

3 _____ go to bed   c) sleepy

4 _____ drowsy   d) awake

5 _____ in an unconscious state   e) exhausted

6 _____ get up   f) nightmare

7 _____ very tired   g) asleep

Exercise 3

Put these events in the most likely order.

1 First, you _____   a) have a dream.

2 Then, you _____   b) go into a deep sleep.

3 So, you _____   c) wake up.

4 After a while, you _____   d) fall asleep.

5 Later, you might _____   e) are tired.

6 Finally, you begin to _____   f) feel sleepy.

Just for fun

Look at this list and decide whether these are good or bad things to do before going to sleep.

	very bad --------- very good				
1 eat a meal	1	2	3	4	5
2 read a book	1	2	3	4	5
3 take a sleeping pill	1	2	3	4	5
4 drink a cup of coffee	1	2	3	4	5
5 do some physical exercises	1	2	3	4	5
6 do your homework	1	2	3	4	5
7 drink a cup of hot milk	1	2	3	4	5

Discuss your answers with someone else. Can you think of other things that help you sleep well, or that stop you falling asleep?

Think about

1 What time do you usually go to bed? Do you fall asleep easily? Do you usually sleep well?

2 Do you usually remember your dreams? Have you had any strange dreams or nightmares that you can remember? Why do you think we dream?

1.4 Washing

Words in context *Read the following passage and do the exercises.*

These days many people start their day by going into the bathroom to **wash**. They turn on a **tap** and hot water runs into the **washbasin**. They pick up a **bar of soap** and wash their hands and face. They take a **towel** to **dry themselves**. Then they put **toothpaste** on their **toothbrush** in order to **brush their teeth**. Not so long ago, however, many homes did not have bathrooms at all. Soap was something that only rich families could afford, and people did not think it was necessary to brush their teeth.

Today we think it is important to be clean, but there was a long period of history when almost no one **had** a **bath** or a **shower**. Queen Isabella of Spain (1451–1504) had only two baths in her life, one on the day she was born and the other on the day she was married. Queen Elizabeth I of England (1533–1603) is said to have had only one bath in her whole life. There was no bath in the White House until 1831 and no bathroom in Buckingham Palace until after 1837. There were even some religious groups who thought that having a bath was a crime against God.

However, wearing **perfume** to smell nice has always been popular, ever since the time of the ancient Egyptians five thousand years ago. Of course, if you think about how often people washed, you will realize why perfume was so necessary.

Exercise 1

Choose the word or phrase in brackets which will make each sentence true according to the information in the passage. Circle the word or phrase as in the example.

Example: (Nowadays/~~In the past~~) most homes (don't/~~didn't~~) have hot water.

1 (Nowadays/In the past) most homes (have/had) bathrooms.

2 (Nowadays/In the past) most people never (brush/brushed) their teeth.

3 (Nowadays/In the past) most people (wash/washed) every day.

4 (Nowadays/In the past) most people (don't/didn't) use soap.

5 (Nowadays/In the past) most kings and queens of Europe (don't/didn't) have baths.

6 (Nowadays/In the past) most people (believe/believed) that it (is/was) important to be clean.

7 (Nowadays/In the past) most people (need/needed) to wear perfume.

Exercise 2

Look at the pictures. Write what each thing is and what it is used for.

	thing	used for
1	_____	_____ your _____
2	_____	_____ yourself
3	_____	_____ yourself
4	_____	_____ a _____

Exercise 3

Match the things on the left with the descriptions on the right.

1 _____ toothpaste		a)	You wash your hands in it.
2 _____ washbasin		b)	Water comes out of it when you turn it on.
3 _____ perfume		c)	You clean your teeth with it.
4 _____ shower		d)	It smells nice.
5 _____ bath		e)	You stand under it.
6 _____ tap		f)	You sit in it.

Dictionary work

The things on the left are used on the different parts of the body on the right. Match each item with a part of the body. More than one answer may be possible, but there is always one best answer. Do as many as you can and then check your answers in a dictionary.

1 _____ lipstick		a)	on a man's face before shaving
2 _____ shaving cream		b)	under the arms
3 _____ shampoo		c)	on the fingernails
4 _____ nail polish		d)	on the hair
5 _____ deodorant		e)	on a man's shaved chin and cheeks
6 _____ aftershave		f)	on the eyes and cheeks
7 _____ make-up		g)	on the mouth

Think about

1 Do you prefer to have a shower or a bath?

2 What do you do to get ready to go out in the morning? How long do you take to get ready?

3 Do you use make-up and perfume? When, why and what kind?

1.5 Housework

Words in context   *Read the following passage and do the exercises.*

Mr and Mrs Turvey both hated housework. They were a very **untidy** couple who never put things away. When they went to bed, for example, they always left their clothes **in a mess** on the floor. Their kitchen was a mess, too. Even though they had a **dishwasher**, they always left the **dirty** dishes in the kitchen sink and only **did the washing-up** when there wasn't a **clean** plate to be found in the house. It was the same with their clothes. They never put them into the **washing machine** until there was nothing else left to wear. The living room always looked as though a bomb had just gone off. There were things everywhere. There was thick **dust** on every piece of furniture and the carpet had not been **cleaned** for weeks.

And the bathroom!

One day, when Mr Turvey couldn't find one of his shoes, and Mrs Turvey couldn't see her face in the bathroom mirror, they decided it was time to get the house cleaned. So they found Marie, a foreign student at a local language school, who needed some extra money.

Marie came to the house and worked all day long. She washed and dried all the clothes. Then she got out the **iron**. She **ironed** the clothes, folded them neatly and put them away. She **swept** all the dust off the floors with a large **broom**. She took a wet **cloth** and **wiped** the dust off every surface in the house and then **polished** the furniture until it was **shining**. She got out the **vacuum cleaner** and cleaned all the carpets. In the kitchen the floor was **filthy**. It was too dirty to wash with a **mop**, so Marie got on her hands and knees and **scrubbed** the dirt off with a **scrubbing brush**. Finally she **made the bed** and, when she had finished, the house looked **spotless**.

Mr and Mrs Turvey came home that evening. There was nothing on the floor. There was no dust on the furniture. The wood was shining and you could smell the **polish**. In their bedroom all their clothes were **neat**, clean and **tidy**. 'So what do you think?' Mrs Turvey asked her husband.

'It looks nice and tidy,' he said, 'but how are we ever going to find anything?'

Exercise 1

Put these pictures into the order in which they are described in the story.

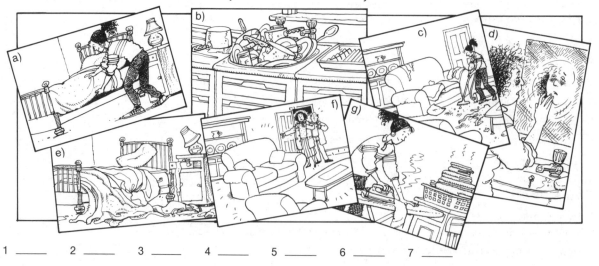

1 _____   2 _____   3 _____   4 _____   5 _____   6 _____   7 _____

Exercise 2

Put these words and phrases into the four sentences.

spotless	dirty	untidy	filthy	in a mess	clean	tidy	neat

1 _____ is similar in meaning to _____

2 _____ is similar in meaning to _____

3 _____ means very, very _____

4 _____ means very, very _____

Exercise 3

What do you use to clean the house? Match the objects in the box with the actions below. More than one answer may be possible, but there is always one best answer.

a) a broom	c) a vacuum cleaner	e) polish	g) a mop	i) a scrubbing brush
b) a dishwasher	d) a washing machine	f) a cloth	h) an iron	

1 _____ to wash clothes

2 _____ to sweep the floor

3 _____ to make clothes smooth

4 _____ to scrub the floor

5 _____ to do the washing up

6 _____ to wash the kitchen floor

7 _____ to clean the carpet

8 _____ to wipe surfaces

9 _____ to make furniture shiny

Just for fun

Imagine you are working for a company that makes products used in housework. It is your job to think of a name and an advertising description for new products.

> *Example:* a new type of vacuum cleaner.
> Name: Vroom
> Sentence: Vroom gets your dirty carpet clean in seconds.

Think of names and write sentences for these products.

1 a washing powder for clothes
2 a furniture polish
3 a liquid for washing dishes
4 a dishwasher
5 an iron

Think about

1 Are you a tidy person?

2 Who does most of the housework in your home? What kind of housework do you do and how often?

3 What kind of housework do you most hate doing? What kind of housework do you least mind doing?

4 Which of the following machines is the most useful for housework: a dishwasher, a washing machine, a vacuum cleaner?

Vocabulary review

1 At home (Units 1.1–1.5)

1.1 Parts of the house

back garden
basement
bathroom
bedroom
ceiling
central heating
chimney
dining room
downstairs
fence
fireplace
floor
front door
front garden
garage
garden
gate
hall
hedge
kitchen
living room
path
roof
storey (*AmE* story)
upstairs
wall
window

1.2 Furniture and furnishings

armchair
ashtray
bench
bookcase
cabinet
carpet
cassette recorder
chair
chest of drawers
coffee table
computer
cupboard
curtain
cushion (*AmE* pillow)
deckchair
desk
dining table
drawer

lamp
linoleum
mat
radio
record
rug
shelf
sofa
stereo system
stool
switch
table
television set
wardrobe

1.3 Sleeping

asleep
awake
bed
  go to bed
blanket
consciousness
deep sleep
dream
drowsy
exhausted
fall asleep
get up
mattress
nightmare
pyjamas (*AmE* pajamas)
pillow
sheet
sleepy
tired
unconsciousness
wake up

1.4 Washing

aftershave
bar of soap
bath (*AmE* bathtub)
  have a bath (*AmE* take a bath)
brush your teeth
deodorant
dry yourself
lipstick
make-up

nail polish
perfume
shampoo
shaving cream
shower
  have a shower (*AmE* take a shower)
tap (*AmE* faucet)
toothbrush
toothpaste
towel
wash
washbasin

1.5 Housework

bed
  make the bed
broom
clean
cloth
dirty
dishwasher
dust
filthy
iron
mess
  in a mess
mop
neat
polish
scrub
scrubbing brush
shine
spotless
sweep
tidy
untidy
vacuum cleaner
washing machine
washing-up
  do the washing-up (*AmE* do the dishes)
wipe

Test yourself 1

Use the words from the **Vocabulary review** to help you fill in the blanks in these sentences. The number of dashes corresponds to the number of letters in the missing word. More than one answer may be possible, but there is always one best answer.

1 Grandfather sat in his favourite _ _ _ _ _ _ _ _ _ in front of the open fire.

2 I'm afraid you can't put your car in my _ _ _ _ _ _ _ . It's full.

3 The rain is coming through the _ _ _ _ _ _ _ in the upstairs bedroom.

4 My aunt's kitchen floor is always _ _ _ _ _ _ _ _ _ . It's so clean you could eat a meal off it.

5 I like the taste of this new _ _ _ _ _ _ _ _ _ _ . I'm going to brush my teeth with it every morning from now on.

6 He decided to _ _ _ _ _ _ every piece of furniture in the house.

7 If you put a _ _ _ _ _ _ _ on that chair, I think you'll find it much more comfortable.

8 It may get very cold tonight, so take another _ _ _ _ _ _ _ for your bed.

9 Do you like the smell of her _ _ _ _ _ _ _ _ ? She always puts it on before she goes out.

10 They played football on a wet, muddy field and came home with _ _ _ _ _ _ clothes.

11 If you leave your umbrella in the _ _ _ _ _ , you'll remember it when you leave the house.

12 Do you prefer to sleep on a hard or a soft _ _ _ _ _ _ _ _ ?

13 She's so untidy. She always leaves her room in a terrible _ _ _ _ _ .

14 Here's a clean _ _ _ _ _ _ . Use it when you get out of the bath.

15 If you keep walking along this _ _ _ _ _ you'll finally come to the farm.

16 Last night I had a terrible _ _ _ _ _ _ _ _ _ _ . I dreamed I was dead.

17 It's very dark in here. Why don't you draw the _ _ _ _ _ _ _ _ _ and let in some light?

18 My grandmother never had a _ _ _ _ _ _ _ _ _ _ _ _ or a washing machine. She washed all the dishes and the clothes by hand in the kitchen sink.

19 We need to buy some more _ _ _ _ _ immediately. There isn't any left in the bathroom and I want to have a bath.

20 If you put the television aerial on the _ _ _ _ _ you'll get a much better picture.

21 After running ten kilometres, she was absolutely _ _ _ _ _ _ _ _ _ _ .

22 Did you put a sleeping pill in that drink? I'm feeling very _ _ _ _ _ _ _ _ .

23 You'll find the light _ _ _ _ _ _ _ by the side of the bed. Turn it on, would you?

24 It took the actor two hours to put on his _ _ _ _ _ - _ _ .

25 You'll find a pencil and some paper in my _ _ _ _ _ .

1.6 Cooking

■■

Words in context   *Read the following passage and do the exercises.*

Here are five simple ways to cook an (EGG)

✖✖ BOILED EGGS ✖✖✖

One of the easiest things to make is a boiled egg. Put an egg into a **saucepan** full of cold water. Put the saucepan on top of the **stove**. Turn on the heat. When the water starts to **boil**, look at your watch. You must boil the water fast for about three to four minutes only. Then remove the egg immediately from the water and serve.

✖✖ EGG SALAD ✖✖

If you want your boiled egg to be hard, then boil the egg in water for about eight to ten minutes. When the egg is cold, **peel** off the egg shell and cut up the egg. **Chop** a little piece of onion with a sharp **knife**. Then **mix** the egg and onion with some mayonnaise. Now you have egg salad. Put this in some fresh bread with some thinly **sliced** tomato and you have a great sandwich.

✖✖ FRIED EGGS ✖✖

Melt a little butter or oil in a **frying pan**. Break the egg into the pan, without breaking its yellow centre. **Fry** it quickly. This is a very popular breakfast dish in Britain and the United States, where it is often served with toast and slices of fried bacon.

✖✖ SCRAMBLED EGGS ✖✖✖

Scrambled eggs are also popular. First, **beat** two eggs together with a little milk. Melt some butter in a frying pan and **pour** in the mixture. **Stir** with a wooden **spoon** and cook until the egg starts to get thick. Make sure you have some buttered toast ready to serve the eggs on.

✖✖ BAKED EGGS ✖✖✖

Eggs can also be **baked** in the **oven**. **Heat** the oven first. Break the egg and pour it into a special oven dish. Add a small spoonful of melted butter or cream, or **grate** some cheese over it, and bake it in the oven for eight to ten minutes.

Exercise 1

Match each picture with one of the ways of cooking an egg described in the passage.

1 _____

2 _____

3 _____

4 _____

5 _____

Exercise 2

Use these words to complete the sentences. You may use each word more than once.

| knife | oven | spoon | saucepan | frying pan | stove |

1 You can bake food in the _____.

2 You can slice food with a _____.

3 You can fry food in a _____.

4 You can heat food on top of the _____.

5 You can mix food up with a _____.

6 You can boil water in a _____.

7 You can chop food with a _____.

8 You can stir food with a _____.

9 You can peel food with a _____.

Exercise 3

Which verbs can be used with these foods?
Match the foods on the left with the actions on the right.

1 milk _____ _____

2 bread _____

3 an orange _____ _____

4 butter _____

5 soup _____ _____

6 a tomato _____ _____ _____

7 cheese _____ _____ _____

8 an onion _____ _____ _____ _____

a) slice

b) grate

c) chop

d) pour

e) melt

f) stir

g) peel

Dictionary work

Decide whether each of these foods is a type of fruit (F), vegetable (V), or meat (M). Do as many as you can and then check your answers in a dictionary.

_____ sausage   _____ ham   _____ grape   _____ pea   _____ bean

_____ pineapple   _____ celery   _____ lamb   _____ cabbage   _____ beef

_____ strawberry   _____ steak   _____ peach   _____ spinach   _____ avocado

_____ turkey   _____ veal   _____ pear   _____ cucumber   _____ plum

Think about

1 Can you cook? Do you enjoy cooking? Why? Why not?
2 What's your favourite food?
3 Which food do you know how to cook best? How do you prepare it?
4 Describe something that people eat every day in your country. How is it prepared?

1.7 Eating

Words in context

Read the following passage and do the exercises.

Before John and Susie Barker went to visit their grandmother, their mother told them that their grandmother thought children should have good table manners. So she wrote out this list of instructions.

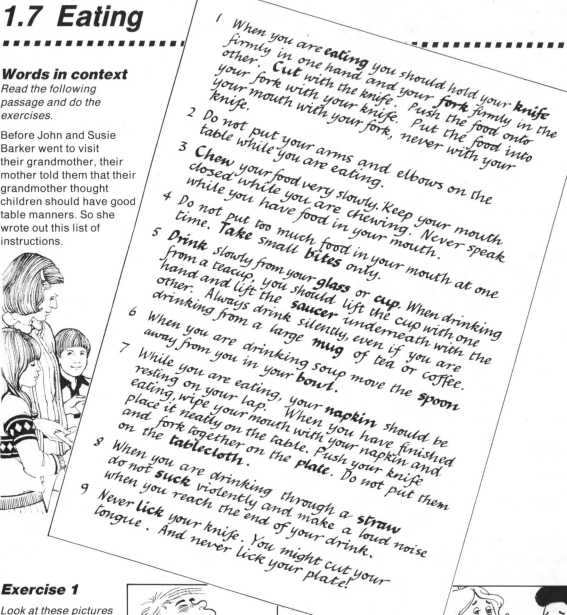

1 When you are **eating** you should hold your **knife** firmly in one hand and your **fork** firmly in the other. **Cut** with the knife. Push the food onto your fork with your knife. Put the food into your mouth with your fork, never with your knife.

2 Do not put your arms and elbows on the table while you are eating.

3 **Chew** your food very slowly. Keep your mouth closed while you are chewing. Never speak while you have food in your mouth.

4 Do not put too much food in your mouth at one time. **Take** small **bites** only.

5 **Drink** slowly from your **glass** or **cup**. When drinking from a teacup, you should lift the cup with one hand and lift the **saucer** underneath with the other. Always drink silently, even if you are drinking from a large **mug** of tea or coffee. When you are drinking soup move the **spoon** away from you in your **bowl**.

6 While you are eating, your **napkin** should be resting on your lap. When you have finished eating, wipe your mouth with your napkin and place it neatly on the table. Push your knife and fork together on the **plate**. Do not put them on the **tablecloth**.

7 When you are drinking through a **straw** do not **suck** violently and make a loud noise when you reach the end of your drink.

8 Never **lick** your knife. You might cut your tongue. And never lick your plate!

Exercise 1

Look at these pictures and write down the number of the rule that has been broken.

a) _____

b) _____

c) _____

d) _____

e) _____

Exercise 2

Match each action on the left with the right noun on the right.

1 You take a bite with _____   a) a spoon.

2 You lick with _____   b) a saucer.

3 You drink soup with _____   c) a mug.

4 You cover your lap with _____   d) your plate.

5 You cover the table with _____   e) your front teeth.

6 You place a cup on _____   f) your back teeth.

7 You suck through _____   g) a bowl.

8 You cut up food with _____   h) a napkin.

9 You put your knife and fork together on _____   i) a knife.

10 You drink hot chocolate out of _____   j) a tablecloth.

11 You put your breakfast cereal in _____   k) your tongue.

12 You chew with _____   l) a straw.

Just for fun

Look at this list and decide whether these are good or bad eating habits. Discuss your answers with someone else.

	very good - - - - - - - - -very bad				
1 eating while you are standing up	1	2	3	4	5
2 a vegetarian diet of fruit and vegetables	1	2	3	4	5
3 eating fried foods	1	2	3	4	5
4 having a large lunch every day	1	2	3	4	5
5 putting salt on your food	1	2	3	4	5
6 drinking three cups of strong coffee every day	1	2	3	4	5
7 drinking fresh orange juice every day	1	2	3	4	5
8 drinking one glass of wine every day	1	2	3	4	5
9 eating very slowly, chewing many times	1	2	3	4	5
10 eating when you are nervous or worried	1	2	3	4	5
11 having no breakfast in the morning	1	2	3	4	5

Think about

1 Compare the table manners and eating habits in your country with those in some other countries that you have visited or heard about.

2 When are the different meal times in your country? What is usually served?

3 Can you describe a healthy diet?

1.8 Keeping food fresh

Words in context   *Read the following passage and do the exercises.*

Food which is left open to the air will **go bad** unless something is done to keep it **fresh**. Some foods go bad very quickly. Milk and other milk products will **go sour** in a few hours. **Raw** meat will **go off** in about a day. Bread, cake and other similar foods will **go stale** in a couple of days. Even many fruits and vegetables will **go rotten** in less than a week. It has always been important, therefore, to find ways of preserving food in order to keep it fresh and **delicious**.

Some methods of preserving food are very old. For example, food was **dried, smoked** or **salted** thousands of years ago. But it was in the early nineteenth century that many of the methods that we use today were invented.

In 1810 a Frenchman, Nicholas Appert, discovered a way of keeping food fresh by putting it in **bottles** and glass **jars**. The **bottled** food was heated and no air was allowed to get in. In 1834, Peter Durand, an Englishman, invented the process of **canning**. He managed to preserve food in air-free metal **tins** (or **cans**). Finally, in 1851, an American called John Gorrie invented the refrigerator, so that food could be kept cold or **frozen**. Together, these three men and their inventions (bottled, **tinned**, and frozen food) have had an enormous effect on what we eat and the way food is bought and sold today.

Exercise 1

Complete the paragraph with words taken from the passage. Use only one word in each blank space.

There are many different ways of preventing food from going (1)_____. Some of them are

(2)_____ of years old. Several important methods were invented in the (3)_____

century. First, a Frenchman discovered a way to keep food (4)_____ in glass (5)_____.

A few years later an Englishman invented canning, in which food is preserved in air-free (6)_____

tins. Finally, John Gorrie invented the (7)_____. In the refrigerator, milk will take much longer to go

(8)_____ and meat will take several days to go (9)_____. And (10)_____

food, which has been kept in the freezer compartment, may not go bad for years.

Exercise 2

The adjectives "bad" or "not fresh" can be used to describe most types of food. Some other adjectives are usually used only with particular types of food. Put each word below in one of the four columns. Looking back at the passage will help you.

| tomatoes | cream | ham | cake | biscuits | chicken | milk | bananas |

sour	**rotten**	**stale**	**off**
1 _____	3 _____	5 _____	7 _____
2 _____	4 _____	6 _____	8 _____

Exercise 3

Match each word in the box with its definition below.

| a) raw | b) dried | c) delicious | d) smoked | e) frozen | f) tinned | g) salted | h) bottled |

1 _____ kept in air-free metal containers

2 _____ kept below 0°C

3 _____ uncooked

4 _____ tasting good

5 _____ kept in air-free glass containers

6 _____ containing no water or liquid

7 _____ heated over a wood fire

8 _____ kept in salt

Dictionary work

Match the containers with the pictures. To help you, the typical contents of each container have also been given. Do as many as you can and then check your answers in a dictionary.

a) a jar (of honey)
b) a bottle (of ketchup)
c) a box (of chocolates)
d) a tin (of peas)
e) a mug (of hot coffee)
f) a glass (of cold water)
g) a packet (of biscuits)
h) a cup (of tea)
i) a kettle (of hot water)
j) a bowl (of cooked rice)
k) a carton (of cream)
l) a bag (of apples)

1 _____   3 _____   5 _____   7 _____   9 _____   11 _____

2 _____   4 _____   6 _____   8 _____   10 _____   12 _____

Think about

1 How many different ways of preserving food can you describe?

2 Are there any ways of preserving food that you think are bad for you? What are they?

3 How and where do you keep the following foods in your home: cheese, milk, bread, tea, coffee, fruit, fresh green vegetables, fresh fruit?

1.9 Clothes

Words in context *Read the following passages and do the exercises.*

Not so long ago, nearly all schoolchildren went to school wearing a school uniform. Boys wore a white **shirt** and a **tie**, a dark **jacket**, grey **trousers** and black **shoes**. Girls used to wear a white **blouse** and a dark, knee-length **skirt**. Today, in many countries, students have a very different kind of uniform. They wear **tennis shoes**, **jeans**, and a **T-shirt**. On a hot day students might even come to class in a pair of **shorts**. Teachers in the past would never have allowed these students into their class. Then the men teachers used to wear a **suit** and tie and most women teachers wore a **dress** or skirt. But when you look inside a classroom today, it is sometimes difficult to tell who are the teachers and who are the students!

(Now answer questions 1, 2 and 3 in Exercise 1.)

People from hot sunny countries often find it difficult to imagine how people who live in a very cold climate can live and work through the winter months. These people manage because they know what to wear in the cold. First, it is very important to keep your head, hands and feet warm. So everyone has a **hat**, thick **gloves** to keep their hands warm, and a pair of long **socks** and strong **boots** for their feet. Of course, you have to have a heavy **overcoat** and you should wear a thick woolly **sweater** under it. A **scarf** around the neck also helps to keep out the cold. What you wear under your clothes is important, too. People who live in cold climates always wear thick **underwear**. Long **underpants** may not look very nice, but they certainly keep your legs warm!

(Now answer questions 4, 5 and 6.)

Exercise 1

Decide whether the following statements are true (T) or false (F) according to the information in the passages.

1 _____ In the past, many female students wore white blouses to school.

2 _____ Today, teachers never allow students to wear jeans to class.

3 _____ Today, many teachers wear the same kind of clothes to school as their students.

4 _____ In many cold countries people wear long socks over their hands and gloves over their feet.

5 _____ In cold weather it's a good idea to wear shorts.

6 _____ In cold weather it's a good idea to wear a scarf.

Exercise 2

Name the articles of clothing in the pictures.

1 _____   2 _____   3 _____   4 _____   5 _____   6 _____

Exercise 3

In chart 1, decide whether the clothes are usually worn above the waist, below the waist,
or both above and below the waist. In chart 2, decide whether the clothes are usually
worn by women or by both men and women. Use crosses (X) to fill the charts.

Chart 1

	above waist	below waist	above and below
1 underpants			
2 suit			
3 dress			
4 tie			
5 shorts			
6 scarf			
7 skirt			
8 underwear			
9 shirt			

Chart 2

	women only	both men and women
1 T-shirt		
2 underwear		
3 jeans		
4 blouse		
5 dress		
6 boots		
7 jacket		
8 gloves		
9 skirt		

Just for fun

Which item of clothing is different from the other three in each group? More than one
answer may be possible. Discuss your answers with someone else.

1 a) shoes   b) socks   c) gloves   d) shirt
2 a) socks   b) jeans   c) trousers   d) shorts
3 a) underpants b) blouse   c) sweater   d) dress
4 a) scarf   b) hat   c) overcoat   d) tie
5 a) tie   b) dress   c) suit   d) T-shirt

Think about

1 How does a typical businessman/woman dress in your country?
2 What do schoolchildren usually wear to school in your country?
3 What clothes do you wear when it is a) very cold b) very wet c) very hot?
4 Describe the traditional clothes or national costume of your country.

1.10 Fashions

Words in context *Read the following passage and do the exercises.*

Spring, summer, autumn, winter: every season there are new clothes and new fashions in the shops. Colours and styles keep changing. One season black is the '**in**' colour, but the next season everyone is wearing orange or pink or grey. One season **tight-fitting** clothes are **fashionable**, and the next season **baggy** clothes are '**in**'.

The length of women's skirts goes up and down from year to year. In the 1960s, mini skirts became very fashionable and a woman could wear a skirt twenty or thirty centimetres above the knee. A few years later, maxi skirts became **trendy** and then you had to wear skirts twenty or thirty centimetres below the knee. Each season there is always a 'correct' length and if your skirt is just a little too long or too short some people will think that you are very **unfashionable**.

Men have similar problems with their shirts. Some years it is fashionable to wear very small collars. Another year small collars become **out-dated** and large **button-down** collars are trendy. Sometimes it even becomes fashionable to wear shirts with no collars at all. A shirt that you once thought was very trendy can look strangely **old-fashioned** a few years later. And your father's shirts, which you always thought were very **conservative** and

traditional, can suddenly seem very **stylish**.

Keeping up with the fashions can be very expensive. So one way to save money is never to throw your old clothes out. If you wait long enough, the clothes that are **out of fashion** today will be back **in fashion** tomorrow. Yesterday's clothes are tomorrow's new fashions.

Exercise 1

Choose the best answer according to the information in the passage.

1 New fashions come out every
   a) year   b) season   c) two years

2 Tight-fitting clothes are
   a) always in fashion   b) sometimes unfashionable
   c) always conservative

3 The fashionable length for a woman's skirt depends on
   a) the year   b) the woman's height
   c) the colour of the skirt

4 You can tell if a man's shirt is trendy by looking at
   a) the collar   b) the buttons   c) the colour

5 It's a good idea to keep your parents' old clothes because
   a) they are conservative
   b) the style might be 'in' again in a few years' time
   c) it is always trendy to wear old-fashioned clothes

Exercise 2

Put these words and phrases into two columns depending on whether they can be used
to describe a modern or an old style.

in fashion	old-fashioned	conservative	out of fashion
stylish	trendy	outdated	in

modern   **old**

_____   _____

_____   _____

_____   _____

_____   _____

Exercise 3

Complete the following sentences as in the example.

Example: A _friendly_ person likes to make friends.

1 A(n) _____ person follows new trends.

2 A(n) _____ person likes to follow traditions.

3 A(n) _____ person doesn't follow fashion.

4 A(n) _____ person likes to wear new styles.

Dictionary work

Match the styles with the pictures. Do as many as you can and then check your answers in a dictionary.

a) short-sleeved	d) checked	g) striped	j) polo neck
b) high-heeled	e) button-down	h) V-neck	k) pleated
c) belted	f) baggy	i) tight-fitting	l) floral

1 _____   2 _____   3 _____   4 _____   5 _____   6 _____

7 _____   8 _____   9 _____   10 _____   11 _____   12 _____

Think about

1 Do you like shopping for clothes? Why? Why not?

2 What clothes are you and your friends wearing at the moment?

3 What styles and colours are fashionable at the moment for men and for women?

4 What was in fashion last year, but is out of fashion this year?

Vocabulary review

1 At home (Units 1.6–1.10)

1.6 Cooking

avocado
bake
bean
beat
beef
boil
cabbage
celery
cucumber
fry
frying pan
grape
grate
ham
heat
knife
lamb
melt
mix
oven
pea
peach
pear
peel
pineapple
plum
pour in
saucepan
sausage
slice
spinach
spoon
steak
stir
stove
strawberry
turkey
veal

1.7 Eating

bite
bowl
chew
cup
drink
eat
fork
glass
knife
lick
mug
napkin
plate
saucer
spoon
straw
suck
tablecloth
teacup

1.8 Keeping food fresh

bad
  go bad
bag
bottle
bottled
bowl
box
canning
carton
cup
delicious
dried
fresh
frozen
glass
jar
kettle
mug
off
  go off
packet
raw
rotten
  go rotten
salted
smoked
sour
  go sour
stale
  go stale
tin/can (AmE can)
tinned/canned (AmE canned)

1.9 Clothes

blouse
boot
dress
glove
hat
jacket
jeans
overcoat
scarf
shirt
shoe
shorts
skirt
sock
suit
sweater
tennis shoe
tie
trousers (AmE pants)
T-shirt
underpants
underwear

1.10 Fashions

baggy
belted
button-down
checked
conservative
fashionable
floral
high-heeled
in adj
in fashion
old-fashioned
out-dated
out of fashion
pleated
polo neck
short-sleeved
striped
stylish
tight-fitting
traditional
trendy
unfashionable
V-neck

Test yourself 2

Use the words from the **Vocabulary review** to help you fill in the blanks in these sentences. The number of dashes corresponds to the number of letters in the missing word. More than one answer may be possible, but there is always one best answer.

1 He likes to follow fashion and always wears _ _ _ _ _ _ _ clothes.

2 When you heat water to 100°C it _ _ _ _ _ _ .

3 My parents always told me to _ _ _ _ _ my food thirty-two times before swallowing it.

4 It's very hot in here. Do you mind if I take off my jacket and _ _ _ _ ?

5 He has some very _ _ _ - _ _ _ _ _ _ _ _ _ _ ideas about what people should and should not wear.

6 Have you ever eaten _ _ _ _ fish? It's very popular in Japan.

7 Instant coffee is very easy to make. Simply put the coffee into a cup and _ _ _ _ _ in the hot water.

8 The friendly dog went up to the little girl and started to _ _ _ _ _ her face.

9 At the moment women are wearing very short skirts, but they probably won't be in _ _ _ _ _ _ _ _ for very long.

10 This bread is incredibly _ _ _ _ _ _ . I almost broke my teeth on it.

11 Do businessmen in your country always wear a _ _ _ _ _ to work?

12 I don't eat _ _ _ _ because in my religion we are not allowed to eat the meat of the pig.

13 In the late 1960s it was very _ _ _ _ _ _ _ _ for men to have long hair.

14 Let's put her Christmas present in this white, cardboard _ _ _ _ .

15 Which _ _ _ _ _ _ _ _ should I put on the table for our guests tonight — the paper ones or the cloth ones?

16 It's very cold outside. Why don't you wear a _ _ _ _ ?

17 The water in the lake is _ _ _ _ _ _ _ because it was so cold last night.

18 The sun is out now and the snow has started to _ _ _ _ _ .

19 The baby fell asleep while it was _ _ _ _ _ _ _ _ milk from its bottle.

20 The honey in that glass _ _ _ _ is made by the bees in this area.

21 She wore a long black evening _ _ _ _ _ _ to the formal party.

22 I'm going to wear my new blue and white _ _ _ _ _ _ _ _ shirt today.

23 The cake has to be in the _ _ _ _ _ for one hour before it's cooked.

24 Your _ _ _ _ _ is empty. Why don't you have some more food?

25 She has just bought an expensive new pair of knee-high leather _ _ _ _ _ _ .

2 At play

2.1 Sports

Words in context *Read the following passage and do the exercises.*

The first modern Olympic games were held in Athens in 1896. There were nine sports: **cycling**, **tennis**, **gymnastics**, **swimming**, **athletics**, **weightlifting**, **rowing**, **wrestling** and **shooting**. **Sailing** was also to have taken place, but had to be cancelled because of bad weather at sea. At that time, as today, most people were interested in the athletics events in the main stadium.

In the first Olympics there were no real team sports. Then, slowly, a few team sports joined the programme. **Football** and **hockey** were the first team sports introduced into the Olympics in London in 1908. Then in 1936, at the Berlin Olympics, the Germans brought in **handball** and the Americans had **basketball** accepted as an Olympic sport.

It often happens that the country that introduces a new sport into the Olympics then goes on to win the gold medals. In 1904, at the Olympics in St. Louis, the Americans introduced **boxing** and won all seven events. Five **horse riding** events were introduced into the 1912 Stockholm Olympics, and

Swedish riders won four of them. And in 1964, at the Tokyo Olympics, two sports which are very popular in Japan were introduced: **judo** and **volleyball**. The Japanese won all three gold medals in the judo, and also won the first women's volleyball competition.

Some new sports have recently been added to the Olympics. In Los Angeles, in 1984, **baseball** was introduced and **windsurfing** became an Olympic sport. In Seoul, Korea, in 1988, there will be **table tennis** for the first time, and tennis will return as an Olympic sport. Unlike tennis, some sports, such as **golf** and **rugby**, have been tried in the Olympics but have never returned.

The Olympic games continue to get bigger and bigger. They also get more and more expensive. Now many people are asking the questions: Are the Olympics too big? Will the Olympics continue? Should the Olympics continue?

Exercise 1

Complete the following chart from the information in the passage above. For each sport fill in the year and place it was first introduced into the Olympics.

1. YEAR_____ PLACE _____
2. YEAR_____ PLACE _____
3. YEAR_____ PLACE _____
4. YEAR_____ PLACE _____
5. YEAR_____ PLACE _____
6. YEAR_____ PLACE _____
7. YEAR_____ PLACE _____
8. YEAR_____ PLACE _____
9. YEAR_____ PLACE _____

Exercise 2

Put each of these sports into one of the three groups.

volleyball	golf	judo	handball	table tennis	tennis
sailing	swimming	cycling	boxing	football	basketball

sports played in teams	**sports that can be played against one other person**	**sports that can be played alone**
_____	_____	_____
_____	_____	_____
_____	_____	_____
_____	_____	_____

Exercise 3

Look at the pictures of sports equipment. Then write the name of the sport in which it is used under the appropriate picture.

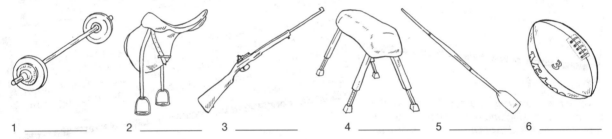

1 _____   2 _____   3 _____   4 _____   5 _____   6 _____

Just for fun

Which sport is different from the other three in each group? There may be more than one possible answer, so discuss your answers with someone else.

1 a) basketball   b) football   c) tennis   d) baseball

2 a) judo   b) volleyball   c) boxing   d) wrestling

3 a) table tennis   b) cycling   c) swimming   d) skiing

4 a) tennis   b) volleyball   c) table tennis   d) basketball

5 a) baseball   b) golf   c) tennis   d) football

6 a) swimming   b) sailing   c) windsurfing   d) rowing

Think about

1 Which sports are you best at? How good are you? How long have you been playing? How often do you play?

2 Do you support a particular team? Which one? How often do you go to a sports event, or do you prefer to watch sports on television?

3 Which sports would you like to learn and why?

4 Do you think the Olympics should continue?

2.2 Actions in sports

Here are some rules taken from a few sports.

Words in context

Read the passages
and do the exercises.

Tennis

After **throwing** the ball up in the air while **serving**, the player's feet must not come down inside the line of the tennis court until he or she has **hit** the ball. As soon as the ball hits the tennis racquet, however, the server can **run** into the court ready to receive the return.

American football

When the quarterback* **passes** the ball to one of his players, the player on the other team who is trying to stop the receiver* from **catching** the ball is not allowed to **tackle** the receiver until the ball touches the receiver's hands. If he tackles too early, he has **committed a foul**. The next play begins where the foul took place.

* A quarterback and a receiver are players in an American football team.

Football

When there is a penalty**, the goalkeeper must have both feet on the goal line and must not move until the player taking the penalty **kicks** the ball. If the goalkeeper starts to **dive** before the ball is touched, then the penalty has to be taken again.

** A penalty is a kick that a player takes from 10 metres in front of the goal after a foul has been committed inside a certain area.

Basketball

After a player **shoots** the ball, nobody is allowed to **jump** and stop the ball from going into the basket if the ball is on its way down into the basket. If this happens, even though the ball has not gone into the basket, the shooting team **scores** two points.

Exercise 1

Look at these pictures and decide if any of the players is breaking one of the rules. Write 'OK' if no rule is broken, and 'Not OK' if a rule is broken.

1 _____

3 _____

2 _____

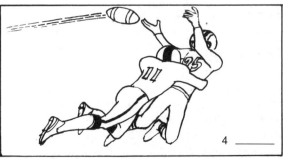

4 _____

Exercise 2

Match each action with one of the definitions below.

a) jump	b) serve	c) kick	d) dive	e) shoot	f) pass	g) tackle	h) commit a foul

1 _____ send (the ball) to another player

2 _____ do something against the rules of the game

3 _____ throw yourself forwards or sideways

4 _____ begin playing for a new point

5 _____ try to get a point or goal

6 _____ take both feet off the ground

7 _____ stop someone from continuing (with the ball)

8 _____ hit with your foot

Exercise 3

Answer these questions with the names of sports from the list on the right.

In which sports . . .?

1 do you pass a ball from one player to another?   _____ _____ _____ _____

2 do you hit a ball (but not with hands or feet)?   _____ _____ _____

3 do you score goals?   _____

4 do you have to jump to catch the ball?   _____ _____

5 do you have to serve?   _____ _____ _____

6 do you have to shoot?   _____ _____

7 do you win by having the lowest score?   _____

8 do you have to tackle?   _____ _____

a) tennis

b) football

c) table tennis

d) golf

e) basketball

f) volleyball

g) American football

Dictionary work

Match the sports terms in the box with an appropriate definition. Do as many as you can and then check your answers in the dictionary.

a) referee	c) bat	e) set	g) match
b) competition	d) course	f) umpire	h) stadium

1 _____ a complete game of football

2 _____ a place where golf is played

3 _____ games played to find the best team

4 _____ person who judges a game of tennis

5 _____ person who judges a game of football

6 _____ something used to hit a ball

7 _____ place where big sports events take place

8 _____ part of a game of tennis or table tennis

Think about

1 Think of your favourite sport. Are there any rules you would like to change? What are they and why?

2 Think of a particular sport and describe the qualities that a good player of that sport needs to have.

3 Which sports do you think are the most dangerous and why?

2.3 Party time

A young man comes up to a young woman at a party and asks her to dance.

HIM: Would you like to dance?
HER: Yes, all right.
HIM: Great party, isn't it? Are you **enjoying yourself**?
HER: Yes, I'm **having a very good time**.
HIM: Who's **giving** this **party**, anyway?
HER: You mean, you weren't **invited**? You're **gatecrashing**?
HIM: No, not really. I came with a friend. He was invited.
HER: Oh, I see. Well, you see that girl over there. That's Jane.
We're **celebrating** her eighteenth birthday.
HIM: Oh, it's a birthday party. Great. Did you give Jane a **present**?
HER: Of course. I gave her several **gifts**. By the way, where's
your friend? Maybe I know him.
HIM: Let me see. There he is. See that guy sitting there all alone?
HER: He doesn't look as if he's **having** much **fun**.
HIM: No, he never enjoys parties. He always finds them **boring**.
HER: You two are very different then, eh?
HIM: Right. I love parties. You can **go wild** and do crazy things. And
you can meet the most **exciting**, interesting people, like you.
HER: Well, thank you and thanks for the dance. Nice meeting you.
HIM: Don't you want to have another dance?
HER: Sorry. I can't. I have to go now and put the candles on Jane's
cake. You see, I'm Jane's mother.

Words in context

*Read the following
dialogue and do
the exercises.*

Exercise 1

The following story describes what happened at the party. Fill in each blank with one word taken from the dialogue.

At a birthday (1)_____ a young man asked a young lady to (2)_____. She accepted.

While they were dancing he asked her if she was (3)_____ herself. She said she was. When he asked

her if she knew whose party it was, the lady asked him if he had been (4)_____. He explained that he

had come with a (5)_____ who had been invited. The lady then told him that the party was to

(6)_____ the birthday of a girl called Jane. The lady then wanted to see who the young man's friend

was. He pointed to a boy sitting alone. The boy didn't look as if he was having (7)_____. The lady said

that the two friends were very (8)_____. The young man agreed, saying that his friend always found

parties (9)_____, but he liked to have a good time and do wild and (10)_____ things.

When the music stopped the lady thanked him for the dance. The young man was upset and wanted to know why she

didn't want to dance any more. The lady then explained that she had to put some candles on Jane's birthday

(11)_____. She said she was Jane's (12)_____.

Exercise 2

Decide if the following pairs of words are similar in meaning or different. If you think they are similar, write S in the blank space. If you think they are different, write D.

1 boring   _____   exciting

2 enjoy yourself   _____   have a good time

3 party   _____   celebration

4 gatecrash   _____   be invited

5 wild   _____   crazy

6 celebrate   _____   invite

7 present   _____   gift

8 be bored   _____   be boring

9 have fun   _____   enjoy yourself

10 candle   _____   cake

Just for fun

Arrange the perfect party. Choose one possibility from each row and arrange the type of party that you usually enjoy best.

night of the week	Mon	Tues	Wed	Thur	Fri	Sat	Sun	
starting time	2pm	4pm	6pm	7pm	8pm	9pm	10pm	12pm
hours	1 2	3 4	5 6	7 8	9	10	11	12
main activity	talking	dancing	playing games		eating	watching TV/film		
number of men	0 1	2 4	8 10	15 20	25	40	60	100
number of women	0 1	2 4	8 10	15 20	25	40	60	100
type of music	none	soft	dance	live music				
type of food	none	sandwiches	peanuts and crisps		a real meal			
type of drink	none	coffee	soft drinks	beer	wine			

Now compare your answers with someone else. See if you can find someone whose answers show that they would like to come to your party!

Think about

1 On what different occasions do people have parties in your country?

2 What do people do at birthday parties in your country?

3 What do people do at New Year's Eve parties in your country?

4 When someone invites you to their home, do you usually take a gift with you? If so, what?

2.4 Places to go and things to do

■■

Words in context

Read the following passage and do the exercises.

Jill is talking on the telephone to her friend Marge, a woman with two children. You only read Jill's side of the conversation, but try to imagine what Marge is saying.

'Hi, Marge. . . Yeah, it's me, Jill. __(a)__ Fine, and you?. . . Good. Listen. I'm just calling to see what you and the kids would like to do tomorrow. You are still coming over, aren't you?. . . Well, I thought we could **go on a trip** somewhere. . . Oh, I don't know. Drive into the country and **go for a walk**. __(b)__ No? Well, would you like to be a tourist for the day and **go sightseeing** in the city? __(c)__ Oh, you think you've **seen** all **the sights**. . . Well, since you are bringing the kids, perhaps we should go to the **circus** or to the **zoo**. There's a new baby elephant that's just been born. __(d)__ The kids are too old for that, you think. Well, are they interested in visiting a **museum** or an **art gallery**? There's a very good **exhibition** of nineteenth-century French painting. __(e)__ No? Boring, eh?. . . Well, what do you think you would all like to do?. . . I see. You want to **go window-shopping**. __(f)__ No, that's fine with me. I don't mind at all. . . No, I'm sure. But what about the evening? I thought we could **go out for dinner**. __(g)__ No, I thought the kids could **stay at home** watching television. . . Well, I thought we could also go to the **cinema**. __(h)__ Really? How about some music? A **concert**? __(i)__ No. The **ballet** or the **opera**?. . . No? The **theatre** to see a Shakespeare play?. . . No. Well, what do you want to do in the evening? __(j)__ You'd like to go to a **disco** and dance and then to a **casino** and play roulette. . . Um, yes, well, no, I've just remembered that I'd promised to visit my mother tomorrow. . . Yes, what a pity. Another time perhaps. . . Bye then. Love to the kids.'

Exercise 1

Find the places in the telephone conversation above where Marge said the following.

1 _____ 'I don't think I feel like listening to music.'

2 _____ 'Do you mind?'

3 _____ 'The kids are much too old for the circus and the zoo.'

4 _____ 'How are you?'

5 _____ 'I'd like to go dancing first and then play roulette.'

6 _____ 'Would we take the children with us to the restaurant?'

7 _____ 'I don't want to go to the country.'

8 _____ 'There's no film on that I really want to see at the moment.'

9 _____ 'I've been sightseeing there plenty of times.'

10 _____ 'No, I'm sure the kids don't want to go to any museum or art gallery.'

Exercise 2

Fill in the following sentences with the most likely preposition (on, to, for, etc.) and/or article (a, an, the). When no article or preposition is necessary, write 0 in the blank.

1 Let's go _____ disco.

2 Let's go _____ sightseeing.

3 Let's visit _____ museum.

4 Let's go _____ shopping.

5 Let's go _____ walk.

6 Let's go _____ trip.

7 Let's go _____ cinema.

8 Let's go out _____ dinner.

9 Let's see _____ sights of Paris.

10 Let's stay _____ home.

Exercise 3

Why would you go to these places? Match each place with the most likely reason for going there.

| a) a disco   b) an art gallery   c) a casino   d) a concert   e) a theatre   f) a zoo   g) a ballet |

1 _____ to see a play

2 _____ to watch people dancing

3 _____ to dance

4 _____ to try to win money

5 _____ to look at the animals

6 _____ to listen to music

7 _____ to look at paintings

Dictionary work

Where are you most likely to be if you can see the following people and things? Write your answers in the spaces below. Do as many as you can and then check your answers in the dictionary.

| a) cages   d) a disc jockey   g) waiters   j) gamblers |
| b) clowns   e) an orchestra   h) an exhibition |
| c) ballerinas f) a big screen   i) a stage |

1 _____ at the theatre

2 _____ at the cinema

3 _____ in a casino

4 _____ at the ballet

5 _____ at the circus

6 _____ at the zoo

7 _____ in a restaurant

8 _____ in a disco

9 _____ in an art gallery

10 _____ at a concert

Think about

1 How often do you go out in the evenings? What do you usually do?

2 How much does it cost to go to the cinema, the theatre, the ballet and the opera in your country in the major cities?

3 Do you enjoy going to discos? Why? Why not?

4 When you visit a new city, do you like to go sightseeing?

2.5 Time for a laugh

Words in context *Read the passage and do the questions.*

Everybody loves a good **joke**. Even children at a very early age start **telling jokes** to their friends. They especially like to **tell riddles** such as 'What has four legs but cannot walk?' and 'What can go up a chimney down but can't go down a chimney up?'

(Answers to riddles are on page 80.)

Some people are very good at telling **funny** stories. When they tell a joke everybody finds it **amusing**. But someone else telling the same joke may not make you laugh. This is because it is not only the end of the joke that has to be funny. A good joke-teller is amusing while telling the whole story.

Some people are **witty** in their normal every-day conversation. They say **humorous** things all the time. They can quickly see two different meanings in the same word and then like to **make puns**. If someone says to them, after their trip to England, 'How did you find London?' they will probably answer by saying something like, 'By turning left at Paris.'

There is another type of humour where people **play jokes on** their friends. They **tease** them by saying untrue things like, 'Someone has just told me that our English teacher is going to give us a test today.' When their friend starts to worry, they laugh and say, 'I'm only **kidding**!' These people love to **pull your leg**. But sometimes when you are having your leg pulled you may not like it because it often seems as if the joker is **making fun of you**, making you look **silly** and ridiculous. And nobody likes to be made fun of. Except, of course, on April 1st. On this day everyone is allowed to play jokes on their friends.

Exercise 1

Use these words to fill in the blanks according to the information in the passage.

kidding	witty	friendly	riddles
joke	silly	true	amusing

1 Children particularly like to tell each other _____.

2 A riddle is a question that has an _____ and unexpected answer.

3 A good _____ is often a good story with a funny ending.

4 A _____ person is someone who says humorous things during a conversation.

5 When you pull someone's leg you may try to make them believe things which are not _____.

6 When you tell someone that you have been pulling their leg, you may say, 'I was just _____.'

7 One way of teasing someone is to pull their leg in a _____ way.

8 When you make fun of someone you might make them do, say or believe something which makes them look

_____.

40

Exercise 2

Which words can go into sentence A and which into sentence B?

1 witty   _____

2 amusing   _____

3 joke   _____   **A** That was a very _____ thing that you said.

4 riddle   _____   **B** That was a very funny _____ .

5 humorous _____

6 pun   _____

Exercise 3

Read the sentences below and say what each speaker is doing.

> a) telling a joke   b) making a pun   c) telling a riddle
> d) pulling someone's leg .   e) making fun of another person

1 _____ 'What is always coming but never arrives?' *(Answer on page 80.)*

2 _____ 'I've just heard your name on the radio. They said you have just won the grand prize in the lottery.'

3 _____ 'Sunday is the strongest day of the week, because all the other days are weekdays.'

4 _____ 'A patient went to see his doctor because he had lost his memory. The doctor asked him, ''How long have you had this problem?'' The patient answered, ''How long have I had what problem?'''

5 _____ 'It was a very good film, full of ideas and very clever, so there's no point in you going to see it.'

Just for fun

Read this joke.

A man walking in the park found a monkey.

He took it to a policeman and asked him what he should do.

'Take it to the zoo,' the policeman told him.

The next day the policeman saw the man still with the monkey.
'I thought I told you to take that monkey to the zoo,' said the policeman.

'I did,' said the man. 'And today I'm taking it to the beach.'

Now you tell a joke or a funny story in English.

Think about

1 What are some different types of a) jokes b) humour?

2 Is there a day in your country when you are expected to pull someone's leg? What sorts of things do you do?

3 In every country there are jokes about people who are said to be very stupid. What are your favourite examples of such jokes?

Vocabulary review

2   At play (Units 2.1–2.5)

2.1 Sports

athletics (*AmE* track and field)
baseball
basketball
boxing
cycling
football/soccer
golf
gymnastics
handball
hockey (*AmE* field hockey)
horse riding
judo
rowing
rugby
sailing
shooting
swimming
table tennis
tennis
volleyball
weightlifting
windsurfing
wrestling

2.2 Actions in sports

bat
catch
competition
course
dive
foul
  commit a foul
jump
kick
match
pass
referee
run
score
serve
set
shoot
stadium
tackle
throw
umpire

2.3 Party time

bored
boring
celebrate
enjoy (yourself)
exciting
fun
  have fun
gatecrash
gift
go wild
good time
  have a good time
invite
party
  give a party
present
  give a present

2.4 Places to go and things to do

art gallery
ballerina
ballet
cage
casino
cinema (*AmE* movies)
circus
clown
concert
dinner
  go out for dinner
disc jockey
disco
exhibition
gambler
museum
opera
orchestra
screen
sights
  see the sights
sightseeing
  go sightseeing
stage
stay at home
theatre
trip
  go on a trip
waiter

walk
  go for a walk
window-shopping
  go window-shopping
zoo

2.5 Time for a laugh

amusing
fun
  make fun of
funny
humorous
joke
  play a joke on
  tell a joke
kid
  be kidding
pull someone's leg
pun
  make a pun
riddle
  tell a riddle
silly
tease
witty

Test yourself 3

Use the words from the **Vocabulary review** to help you fill in the blanks in these sentences. The number of dashes corresponds to the number of letters in the missing word. More than one answer may be possible but there is always one best answer.

1 I hate it when people _ _ _ _ _ _ me. I think they are making fun of me.

2 I'd like to go on a _ _ _ _ _ _ _ _ _ _ _ _ _ tour of all the capital cities of Europe.

3 I bought myself a very good bicycle so that I could do a lot of _ _ _ _ _ _ _ _ at the weekends.

4 In the last football match I _ _ _ _ _ _ _ six goals.

5 In this theatre the _ _ _ _ _ _ is in the middle and the audience sits all the way around it.

6 How many people did you _ _ _ _ _ _ to the party?

7 You didn't really get married yesterday, did you? Come on, you're _ _ _ _ _ _ _ _, aren't you?

8 My cousin has started doing _ _ _ _ _ _ _ _ _ _ _ _ _ _ _ . He wants to build up his muscles.

9 Our team reached the final of the _ _ _ _ _ _ _ _ _ _ _ by winning six matches.

10 Did you think that _ _ _ _ _ was funny? I couldn't understand it.

11 It helps to be tall if you want to play _ _ _ _ _ _ _ _ _ _ _ .

12 Let's go on a _ _ _ _ _ to the countryside this weekend.

13 How many birthday _ _ _ _ _ _ _ _ did you get this year?

14 She's so _ _ _ _ _ _ . Sometimes when I'm talking to her I just can't stop laughing.

15 In both tennis and volleyball you are not allowed to touch the _ _ _ during the game.

16 'Did you _ _ _ _ _ your summer holidays?'
    'Yes, very much.'

17 Do you think _ _ _ _ _ _ _ is more difficult at sea or on a lake?

18 How do you _ _ _ _ _ _ _ _ _ _ the New Year in your country?

19 You should read this. It's very _ _ _ _ _ _ _ _ . I think you'll laugh.

20 He gave up playing football, but continued his interest in the sport by becoming a _ _ _ _ _ _ _ _ .

21 There's a very interesting exhibition at the _ _ _ _ _ _ _ this month.

22 The footballer received the ball in front of the goal and everyone shouted, '_ _ _ _ _ _ !'

23 It was a very _ _ _ _ _ _ _ _ football match. The final score was 0-0.

24 _ _ _ _ _ _ _ _ _ _ _ can be a very beautiful sport to watch. It's almost like ballet dancing.

25 How much money did you lose gambling at the _ _ _ _ _ _ _ last night?

2.6 Entertainers

■■

Words in context *Read the following passages and do the exercises.*

Have you ever stood in front of a large group of people and had to speak or perform? Some people perform in front of an audience every single day. They are the professional **entertainers** and their work is not always easy.

Every night in the theatre, **actors** and **actresses** have to remember thousands of words. Every night in concert halls and night clubs, **musicians** try hard to make no mistakes when they play their music. **Singers** worry about singing the right notes. **Magicians** are nervous about making mistakes, worrying that one day a magic trick or a card trick will not work. Perhaps circus **clowns** and night club **comedians**, however, have the hardest job of all. They have to make people laugh every day with well-told jokes and funny acts. No, being an entertainer is not such an easy way to make a living.

A lot of people also think that all entertainers are well-paid, but not everyone in the entertainment world makes a lot of money. Of course, there are a few **film stars, pop stars** and **television personalities** who make millions of pounds every time they open their mouths. There are also a few famous **film directors** who make a lot of money telling actors and actresses how to speak and where to stand. Some of the best **stunt men** and **women** are also well-paid for jumping out of moving cars and off high buildings, and for all the other dangerous things that they have to do. However, there are also thousands and thousands of actors, actresses and singers who find it very difficult to get work acting and singing. Then, when they do find work, most of them earn very little money.

Exercise 1

Decide if the following statements are true (T) or false (F) according to the information in the passage.

1 _____ An audience is a group of people who watch a performer.

2 _____ Actors and actresses have to have good memories.

3 _____ Many performers worry that something may go wrong.

4 _____ Clowns and comedians don't want their audiences to laugh.

5 _____ It is easy to make money as an entertainer.

6 _____ The best-paid entertainers are, in fact, not very famous.

7 _____ Stunt men and women can make a lot of money.

8 _____ Although many actors are unemployed, they are usually well-paid when they are working.

Exercise 2

Match each picture
to a person
working in the
entertainment industry.

| film director | actress | magician | stunt man | clown |

1 _____ 2 _____ 3 _____ 4 _____ 5 _____

Exercise 3

Match each entertainer with a description of his or her work.

1 A comedian _____   a) does clever tricks with his or her hands.

2 A film star _____   b) makes records.

3 An actor _____   c) has an important part in a film.

4 A musician _____   d) tells jokes.

5 A pop star _____   e) does dangerous things.

6 A magician _____   f) plays in an orchestra, group or band.

7 A stunt woman _____   g) performs in plays on the stage.

Just for fun

Take any letter of the alphabet. Then see how quickly you can find a famous person to
fill each box in the chart. Each person's last name must begin with the same letter. See
if you can fill in the chart more quickly than your friends.

Each name will begin with the letter _____

1 a comedian	
2 a male pop star	
3 a female pop star	
4 a film director	
5 a famous male film star	
6 a famous female film star	

Think about

1 Have you ever performed? What did you do? Did you enjoy doing it?

2 Would you like to be famous like a film star or a pop star? Why? Why not?

3 Who are your favourite film stars, pop stars, comedians and television personalities?

4 What magic tricks can you perform?

2.7 Music

Concerts at the GILMOUTH HIPPODROME

Words in context

Read the passages and then do the exercises.

June 22nd — **LAS PALOMAS**
This South American **group** play the traditional **tunes** and sing the popular **folk** songs of Peru and Bolivia.

June 30th — **THE BAD BAD BOYS**

Punk music from one of the new wave of punk **bands** coming out of California.

July 7th — **RONNIE PARQUETTE**
One of the world's greatest **jazz** musicians excites you with the wonderful **rhythms** of his **saxophone**.

July 14th — **"ELVIS LIVES!"**
He looks like Elvis! He sings like Elvis! Jimmy Wilkes creates the great sound of the great **rock** singer – Elvis Presley.

July 19th — **AN EVENING OF CLASSICAL MUSIC**
The Vienna Orchestra play some of your favourite tunes – the timeless **melodies** of Mozart, Strauss and Beethoven.

July 22nd — **JAMAICA INN**

This West Indian band plays **reggae** music that will make you want to get up and dance. Listen and dance to the great reggae **beat**.

July 28th — **"SIXTIES NIGHT!"**
Pop music from the 1960s played by *Sam and the Band*. Remember the songs and sounds of the pop greats – the Beatles, the Beach Boys, the Hollies and many many more.

Exercise 1

Match the names of the performers with the type of music that they play.

1 _____	The Bad Bad Boys	a)	pop music
2 _____	Jimmy Wilkes	b)	jazz
3 _____	Jamaica Inn	c)	punk music
4 _____	Las Palomas	d)	classical music
5 _____	Sam and the Band	e)	rock
6 _____	The Vienna Orchestra	f)	reggae
7 _____	Ronnie Parquette	g)	folk music

Exercise 2

Which drawings represent the words below?

band	rhythm	tune	melody	beat	group

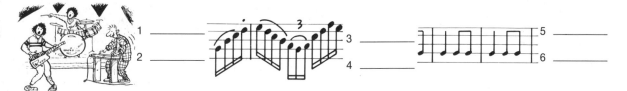

1 ———
2 ———
3 ———
4 ———
5 ———
6 ———

Exercise 3

Complete this chart by putting a cross (X) next to the characteristics of each type of music.

	pop	punk	folk	reggae	jazz	classical
1 often played by a big orchestra in a concert hall						
2 often played by young people with guitars in a group						
3 often played by young people with brightly coloured hair						
4 often simple tunes which are popular for a short time						
5 music coming originally from black American musicians						
6 music of a specific region, popular for a very long time						
7 music with a strong regular rhythm, originally from Jamaica						
8 music which is popular for dancing in discos						
9 often played freely, not following written music						

Dictionary work

Match the names of the musical instruments to the pictures.

a) guitar   b) organ   c) saxophone   d) violin   e) piano   f) trumpet   g) flute   h) drums

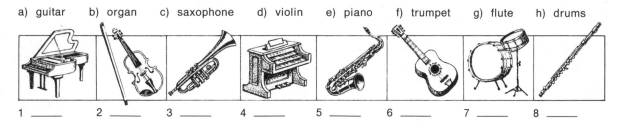

1 _____   2 _____   3 _____   4 _____   5 _____   6 _____   7 _____   8 _____

Think about

1 What type of music do you most like to listen to when you are a) with friends
   b) relaxing alone c) dancing? What about your parents' generation?

2 Do you play a musical instrument? How long have you played? How well do you play?

3 What is a new popular type of music at the moment? Can you describe it?

2.8 Television

■■■

Words in context *Read about the television programmes on Monday evening on Channels 1, 2 and 3 and then do the exercises.*

	Channel 1		Channel 2		Channel 3	
7:00	The <u>News</u>	Read by Janet Flower.	The Million Dollar Minute	A **documentary** about **commercials** in the United States, where a T.V. **advertisement** can cost $1m during prime time T.V.	Globe	Nightly **soap opera** that takes you into the lives and loves of people on a major London newspaper.
7:30	Name that <u>Movie</u>	The popular weekly **quiz show** in which contestants show how much they know about the cinema.			World News on Monday	Alice Tamms and John Johnson bring you the latest news from around the world.
			(7:45) Chicago Cops	New **detective series** set in Chicago. McTaggart and Smith are the two cops who fight crime in the windy city.		
8:00	<u>Film</u> of the Week	Jaws (1975). Film about a shark that terrorizes a small tourist resort.			Life with Susan	The first of a new weekly **comedy** series about a father who lives alone with his daughter Susan.
8:30					Tom and Jerry	More comedy with a half-hour of **cartoons**, showing your favourite cat and mouse.
			(8:45) News and Weather	Read by Arthur Small.		
9:00			Sport on Two	The **sports programme** that takes you back to some of the greatest moments in sports history. Tonight: The World Cup Final of 1966.	Night of Death	1987 film made for television. A killer goes crazy in the London underground.
9:30	Night Time	The nightly **current affairs** programme hosted by Gordon Foster, who looks at the latest in world events.				
10:00	Tennis	The best match from today's play at the Paris Open Tennis Tournament.			Face to Face	In Roger Baltham's **talk show** this week he interviews the film star Gloria Braggio.

Exercise 1

On which channels can you watch the following types of programmes on Monday evening?

1 a sports programme	a) 1 & 2	b) 2 & 3	c) 1 & 3	d) 1, 2, & 3
2 the news	a) 1 & 2	b) 2 & 3	c) 1 & 3	d) 1, 2, & 3
3 a comedy show	a) 1	b) 2	c) 3	d) 1, 2, & 3
4 a film	a) 1	b) 1 & 2	c) 1 & 3	d) 1, 2, & 3
5 a quiz show	a) 1	b) 2	c) 3	d) 2 & 3
6 a detective series	a) 1	b) 2	c) 3	d) 1 & 2
7 a current affairs programme	a) 1	b) 2	c) 3	d) 1 & 3
8 a talk show	a) 1	b) 2	c) 3	d) 2 & 3

Exercise 2

What type of television programme are you probably watching if you see the following?
Match the descriptions on the left with the programmes on the right.

1 _____ People trying to answer questions

2 _____ Actors doing and saying funny things

3 _____ People discussing politics

4 _____ The animal life of Antarctica

5 _____ Guns, murder and police

6 _____ A long interview with a famous person

7 _____ The everyday lives of the same group of people

8 _____ Characters played by moving drawings, not people

9 _____ Someone talking about a new soap powder

10 _____ A person telling you what happened today

a) a detective series

b) a commercial

c) a soap opera

d) a comedy series

e) a talk show

f) a current affairs programme

g) a nature documentary

h) the news

i) a quiz show

j) a cartoon

Just for fun

Imagine you can choose the programmes to go on two television channels in the
evening. Fill in the chart below with the names of the television programmes and say
what types they are (news, sports, talk show, etc.).

	CHANNEL 1	CHANNEL 2
7:00	_____	_____
8:00	_____	_____
9:00	_____	_____
10:00	_____	_____

Think about

1 How much time do you spend watching television? What are your favourite types of
   programmes?

2 How many hours a day is television on in your country? How many different television
   channels do you have? What is the difference between them?

3 What are the good and bad things about television?

2.9 Reading

Words in context *Read the following passage and do the exercises.*

Some people think that as more and more people have televisions in their homes, fewer and fewer people will buy **books** and **newspapers**. Why read an **article** in the newspaper, when the TV news can bring you the information in a few minutes and with pictures? Why read a **novel**, when a **play** on television can tell you the same story with colour, picture and action?

Why read the **biographies** of famous men and women, when an hour-long television programme can tell you all that you want to know?

Television has not killed reading, however. Today, newspapers and **magazines** sell in very large numbers. And books of every kind are sold more than ever before. Books are still a cheap way to get information and entertainment. Although some books with hard covers are expensive, many books are published today as **paperback** books, which are reasonably cheap. A paperback novel, for example, is almost always cheaper than an evening at the cinema or theatre, and you can keep a book forever and read it many times.

Books in the home are a wonderful source of knowledge and pleasure and some types of books should be in every home. Every home should have a good **dictionary**. Every home should have an **atlas** of the world, with large clear maps. It might be expensive, but a good **encyclopedia** is useful, too, because you can find information on any subject. In addition, it is useful to have on your bookshelves other **non-fiction** books such as history books, science **textbooks**, cookery books, books about medicine and health, etc. It is equally important to have some **fiction** on your shelves, too. Then you can relax with a good **story**, or from time to time you can take a book of **poems** off your shelves and read the thoughts and feelings of your favourite poets.

Exercise 1

Choose the best answer according to the information in the passage.

1 Which is easier to get the news from?
  a) a newspaper   b) the television

2 Which is usually quicker?
  a) to read a biography of a famous person
  b) to watch a television programme about a famous person

3 Which is usually cheaper?
  a) a paperback   b) an evening at the cinema

4 Which is usually cheaper?
  a) a paperback   b) a hardcover book

5 Which is it most important to have in your home?
  a) non-fiction books, such as a dictionary and an encyclopedia
  b) fiction, such as novels, short stories and books of poems
  c) a mixture of both good non-fiction and your favourite fiction

Exercise 2

Which of the following are non-fiction and which are fiction? Put the words into the appropriate column.

| atlas | novel | short story | textbook | play | dictionary | encyclopedia | poem |

fiction   **non-fiction**

_____ | _____

_____ | _____

_____ | _____

_____ | _____

Exercise 3

Match the words on the left with their definitions on the right.

1 _____ an article

2 _____ an atlas

3 _____ a biography

4 _____ a novel

5 _____ a textbook

6 _____ a dictionary

7 _____ a poem

8 _____ a paperback

9 _____ a magazine

a) a book that is used to study a school subject

b) a publication that comes out weekly or monthly

c) a book with maps of the world

d) usually a cheap book with a soft cover

e) a story about a real person

f) a piece of writing in a newspaper

g) a book of word definitions

h) usually a short piece of writing expressing a deep feeling or thought

i) a story about people who are not real

Dictionary work

Decide if the following words have to do with newspapers or textbooks. Write (N) next to the newspaper words and (T) next to the textbook words. Do as many as you can and then check your answers in the dictionary.

1 ____ index	4 ____ headline	7 ____ crossword	10 ____ glossary
2 ____ column	5 ____ title	8 ____ cartoon	11 ____ editorial
3 ____ chapter	6 ____ classified ads	9 ____ appendix	12 ____ introduction

Think about

1 What newspapers and magazines do you read in your country? Describe them and say how often you read them.

2 What type of books do you like to read? Who are your favourite writers?

3 How many books do you read in a year? How many do you buy?

2.10 The art of conversation

Words in context *Read the passages and do the exercises.*

Alex and Chris love to **chat** for hours on the telephone. Their favourite topic is their neighbours. Here is an example of the two of them **gossiping** on the telephone. 'Did you see the new couple who moved in next door to me? Do you think they're married? You know, last night they were **having** a terrible **argument**. They were **shouting** at each other so loud I could hear almost every word through the walls. So I think they must be married, don't you? He's very handsome, don't you think? And have you seen her car? Must be rich. And you know something else, either she's a little fat, or I think she's going to have a baby.' (Now answer question 1, Exercise 1.)

For the fiftieth time in his life Professor Marchant stood up to **give** his **lecture** on the causes of the First World War. He started, 'Today I'm going to **discuss** with you the causes of the First World War. . .' Soon, as usual, most of the students were sleeping. The students who were awake could not take good notes, because they could only hear clearly one or two words in every sentence. You see, Marchant was not only boring, but he **mumbled** a great deal when he spoke. It was as if he always had a potato in his mouth when he was speaking. (Now answer question 2.)

For the first time in his life, Mr Parrot had to **give** a **speech**. His daughter had just got married and there were a hundred guests at the wedding party waiting to hear his words. He had practised his speech for hours until he could say it perfectly and he had five pages of notes to help him. He stood up and started. 'Th-th-th-th-thank you f-f-f-f-f c-c-c-c-coming' he **stuttered**, and then sat down very red in the face. (Now answer question 3.)

The two boys sat **whispering** to each other at the back of the classroom. In very quiet voices they were having a very interesting **conversation** about football, girls, parents and even school. Meanwhile, Mrs Garret talked and talked and talked about William Shakespeare. At the end of the lesson, Mrs Garret looked at the two boys and said, 'Next time you have a conversation in my class, please don't whisper. Talk a little louder so that we can all enjoy what you are saying.' (Now answer question 4.)

Exercise 1

Decide which is the best answer according to the information in the passages.

1 Alex and Chris love to talk about
   a) themselves
   b) people they know
   c) people in the news

2 None of the students could take good notes because
   a) they were sleeping
   b) the professor was boring
   c) the professor spoke unclearly

3 Mr Parrot only said four words because
   a) he had prepared a short speech
   b) he was very nervous
   c) he always had problems saying the first letters of a word

4 The next time the boys were in her class, Mrs Garret really wanted them
   a) not to whisper   b) to talk more clearly
   c) not to have a conversation

Exercise 2

Match the situations with the most likely way of talking.

1 You are talking to someone in a library. You are _____

2 You and your friends are talking about politics. You are _____

3 Someone is talking in their sleep. He is _____

4 Your professor is telling you about the history of Europe. She is _____

5 The President is talking to the country on TV. He is _____

6 A parent is angry with her son. She is _____

7 You are disagreeing with your friend about politics. You are _____

8 You are cold and nervous. You are _____

9 You are talking with a friend about the weather. You are _____

10 Your neighbours are talking about your friends. They are _____

a)	shouting
b)	mumbling
c)	chatting
d)	gossiping
e)	whispering
f)	giving a lecture
g)	discussing
h)	having an argument
i)	stuttering
j)	giving a speech

Dictionary work

Match the sentences with their functions as in the example. Do as many as you can and then check your answers in the dictionary.

a)	accuse	c)	apologize	e)	warn	g)	advise	i)	forgive	k)	exaggerate
b)	beg	d)	confess	f)	deny	h)	promise	j)	agree	l)	threaten

Example: 'Waiter, my soup is cold.' Function: complain

1 _____ 'It doesn't matter that you stole my book.'

2 _____ 'I didn't do it. I didn't steal any money.'

3 _____ 'I did it. I stole the money.'

4 _____ 'Please, please, please help me.'

5 _____ 'If you don't give me the money, I'll kill you.'

6 _____ 'I really think you ought to get a new job.'

7 _____ 'Be careful.'

8 _____ 'This is the worst, worst day in my whole life.'

9 _____ 'I will help you. I really will.'

10 _____ 'You did it. You stole the money.'

11 _____ 'You're right.'

12 _____ 'I'm sorry.'

Think about

1 Have you ever given a speech? When? What was it about? Were you nervous?

2 What are the qualities of a good speaker or lecturer?

3 Do you have a lot of arguments in your family? What are they usually about?

4 What is the difference between   a) a gossip and a conversation
   b) a conversation and a discussion   c) a discussion and an argument?

Vocabulary review

2 At play (Units 2.6–2.10)

2.6 Entertainers

actor
actress
clown
comedian
entertainer
film director
film star
magician
musician
pop star
singer
stunt man/woman
television personality

2.7 Music

band
beat
classical
drums
flute
folk
group
guitar
jazz
melody
orchestra
organ
piano
pop
punk
reggae
rhythm
rock
saxophone
trumpet
tune
violin

2.8 Television

advertisement
cartoon
channel
comedy
commercial
current affairs
detective series
documentary
film (*AmE* movie)
news
programme (*AmE* program)
quiz show
series
show
soap opera
talk show

2.9 Reading

appendix
article
atlas
biography
book
cartoon
chapter
classified ad
column
crossword
dictionary
editorial
encyclopedia
fiction
glossary
headline
index
introduction
magazine
newspaper
non-fiction
novel
paperback
play
poem
story
textbook
title

2.10 The art of conversation

accuse
advise
agree
apologize
argument
   have an argument
beg
chat
confess
conversation
   have a conversation
deny
discuss
exaggerate
forgive
gossip
lecture
   give a lecture
mumble
promise
shout
speech
   give a speech
stutter
threaten
warn
whisper

Test yourself 4

Use the words from the **Vocabulary review** to help you fill in the blanks in these sentences. The number of dashes corresponds to the number of letters in the missing word. More than one answer may be possible but there is always one best answer.

1 When I want to relax, I really like to listen to eighteenth-century _ _ _ _ _ _ _ _ _ music.

2 I always wonder whether _ _ _ _ _ _ _ _ _ _ write their own jokes.

3 Turn on the _ _ _ _ _ . I've just heard there's been a terrible air crash.

4 I have no idea what to do next. Could you possibly _ _ _ _ _ _ _ me?

5 'Haven't you finished that novel I lent you?'
  'Almost. I've just started the last _ _ _ _ _ _ _ .'

6 How many television _ _ _ _ _ _ _ _ do you have in your country?

7 When _ _ _ music first started, many parents didn't want their children to listen to it.

8 Is there an _ _ _ _ _ _ in that textbook? I can't find one at the back.

9 What was the name of the _ _ _ _ _ _ _ _ who played Lady Macbeth at the Globe Theatre?

10 Do you get nervous when you have to give a _ _ _ _ _ _ _ in front of a lot of people?

11 Our band has a singer and three guitarists, but we still need someone to play the _ _ _ _ _ _ .

12 He's one of the best _ _ _ _ _ _ _ _ _ _ I've ever seen. I've no idea how he does his tricks.

13 What's the _ _ _ _ _ _ _ _ on the front page of today's newspaper?

14 There's a new detective _ _ _ _ _ _ _ starting on television tomorrow night.

15 Good public speakers never _ _ _ _ _ _ _ . They always speak very clearly.

16 Children all over the world have enjoyed the films and cartoons of the great _ _ _ _ _ _ _ _ _ _ _ _ _ _ , Walt Disney.

17 Most people think that Shakespeare only wrote plays, but he also wrote many wonderful _ _ _ _ _ _ _ .

18 Last night there was a very interesting _ _ _ _ _ _ _ _ _ _ _ _ _ _ _ on television about mountain climbing.

19 'How important are the words in a pop song?'
  'Not very. I think people most want a good _ _ _ _ _ to dance to.'

20 If you don't want anyone else to hear, _ _ _ _ _ _ _ _ _ in my ear.

21 Children always love the circus and especially the _ _ _ _ _ _ _ .

22 Who is the most popular _ _ _ _ _ _ in your country and what sort of music do they play?

23 I always like to _ _ _ _ _ with the person next to me on a long train or plane journey.

24 I couldn't find one interesting article in last month's _ _ _ _ _ _ _ _ _ .

25 What sort of _ _ _ _ _ _ _ _ _ _ _ _ _ _ _ _ do you think are most effective in selling a company's product?

3 At work

■■■■■■■■■■■■■■■■■■■■■■■■■■■■■■

3.1 Jobs

Words in context *Read the following passages and do the exercises.*

 My name is Martha Glass. I'm thirty-nine years old and I'm a **doctor**. I chose the medical **profession** because I wanted to help people and at the same time make good money. When I was younger I wanted to become a **teacher** or a **nurse**, but I soon realized there wasn't much money in either of those professions. My parents didn't help me much, because they didn't want me to have a **career** at all. They wanted me to do what so many other girls did. They wanted me to become a **secretary**, marry the **boss**, have kids and stay at home. Well, I got married, and I had kids, but I have my career as well.

 My name is George Rushton. I'm a **businessman**. I'm fifty years old and I've been working for the same company for twenty-five years. I think I've had a very successful career. I started work with the company as a poorly paid **clerk**. I was one of those nine-to-five **white-collar office workers** who spend all day with a pencil in one hand and a telephone in the other. I hated it. So I got transferred to sales and became one of the company's **sales representatives**. I travelled all over the country selling the company's products and became the most successful **salesperson** on the staff. In ten years I have been promoted to **manager** of the sales department. In another ten years I hope to retire with a good pension.

 Hi. I'm Billy. I left school when I was sixteen. I didn't have any qualifications. I just wanted to earn some money. I got a **job** in a factory. I didn't mind being a **blue-collar** worker. All I wanted was enough money to take my girlfriends out on a Saturday night. But then they got robots in to do my job and I was **out of work**. I was out of work for sixteen months. It's terrible being **unemployed**. The days seem so long. I finally got a job as an **unskilled** labourer, working for a builder. I'm twenty-five now. I suppose I should go to night classes and get some extra training so that I can earn more money as a **skilled** worker.

Exercise 1

Answer the following questions according to the information in the passages.

	Martha	George	Billy	No one
1 Who had a white-collar job for a while?				
2 Who works in a profession?				
3 Who wanted to become a secretary?				
4 Who is unemployed at the moment?				
5 Who is an unskilled worker?				
6 Who was a successful salesperson?				
7 Who wanted a different career as a child?				
8 Who married the boss?				
9 Who has no career?				
10 Who was out of work for a while?				

Exercise 2

Find the words and phrases which are similar in meaning.

blue-collar worker	factory worker	unemployed	boss
out of work	office worker	manager	white-collar worker

1 _____ is similar in meaning to _____.

2 _____ is similar in meaning to _____.

3 _____ is similar in meaning to _____.

4 _____ is similar in meaning to _____.

Exercise 3

Decide what kinds of jobs the following are. Put a cross (X) in the correct box.

	professional worker	white-collar worker	skilled worker
1 engineer			
2 secretary			
3 bank cashier			
4 architect			
5 teacher			
6 mechanic			
7 lawyer			
8 computer repair person			
9 office manager			
10 hairdresser			

Just for fun

What do you think is most important to you in a job and what is least important? Put the following in order (from 1 to 6). Discuss your answer with someone else and explain your order.

_____ flexible working hours   _____ contact with interesting people   _____ chance to travel

_____ long holidays   _____ nice, quiet, attractive work space   _____ a good pension

What are some other things that you think make a good job?

Think about

1 Have you ever had a job? How many? What kind were they?

2 What are some good jobs to have and why? What are the worst jobs?

3 Would you rather have an uninteresting well-paid job or an interesting but poorly-paid job?

4 Are there many unemployed people in your country? Who? Young? Old? People in the north or south? How can they find jobs?

3.2 Farm work

■■■

Words in context *Read the description of a typical year on a farm in Europe and then do the exercises.*

Spring

Spring is the time to prepare the earth for **planting**. First, the farmer **fertilizes** his **fields** with cow or horse **manure** or a chemical fertilizer. Then he **ploughs** the earth, turning it over and mixing in the fertilizer to provide a rich **soil** for the **crops**. Later, when the days are a little longer and the sun has warmed the earth, it is time to plant the seeds. Meanwhile, if the farmer keeps animals, spring is the time when the animals are giving birth, and both mothers and their young ones have to be watched and cared for.

Summer

After planting, the farmer waits and watches. He watches the weather, hoping for enough rain and enough sun. He **waters** the young plants and watches carefully for signs of plant disease and the attacks of insects. Many farmers **spray** their fields with chemicals to keep away disease and harmful insects. With water, sun, care and protection the plants grow strong and healthy.

Winter

The days are getting shorter and shorter. The harvested crops are sold in the markets or **stored** in the **barns**, ready to **feed** the animals through the winter months. The farmer **chops** wood, preparing to keep his house warm through the long cold winter nights. And when winter finally comes, it is a time for planning, for deciding where and what to plant next year. For soon it will be spring again and the cycle of planting, growing and harvesting will start again.

Autumn

This is the busiest time of the year. Now the crops in the fields are ready to **harvest**. The fruit is ready to **pick**. It is time to **gather** in the vegetable crops and to **reap** the grass crops, such as **wheat** and corn. The farmers have to work quickly. Often it is necessary to call in extra workers to work in their fields and bring in the crops. Work starts when the sun rises and finishes when the sun sets. The days are hard and long. But when the job is done, it is time for celebrating, for dancing, eating, drinking and having fun.

Exercise 1

Fill in the chart according to the information above. Decide whether a job is done on the farm in spring, summer, autumn or winter.

	spring	summer	autumn	winter
1 The fields are planted.				
2 The fruit is picked.				
3 The crops are sprayed.				
4 The corn is reaped.				
5 The fields are planned.				
6 The wood is chopped.				
7 The crops are stored in the barns.				
8 The fields are ploughed.				
9 The fields are watered.				
10 The fields are fertilized.				

Exercise 2

Put these events in the order in which they usually occur.

1 First, the farmers _____

2 Then, they _____

3 After that, they _____

4 Perhaps they have to _____

5 Finally, it's time to _____

6 Then they have to _____

7 Now they can _____

a) harvest the crops.
b) fertilize their fields.
c) feed the animals in the winter.
d) store the crops.
e) plant the crops.
f) plough the fields.
g) spray the crops.

Exercise 3

Match the verbs on the left with each noun on the right in order to make a job that you are likely to find on a farm.

	the horses	the earth	the wood	the crops	the corn	the grapes	the chickens	the vegetables	the fields
plough									
harvest									
chop									
feed									
pick									
water									

Dictionary work

Match the words in the box with the definitions below.

a) a hen	c) a tractor	e) a bull	g) manure	i) a vineyard	k) a shepherd
b) a field	d) a barn	f) wheat	h) an axe	j) soil	l) cattle

1 _____ earth; the place where plants grow

2 _____ a sharp tool for chopping trees

3 _____ a male animal that can be dangerous

4 _____ a farm animal that lays eggs

5 _____ a person on a farm who looks after the sheep

6 _____ a powerful motor vehicle used on a farm

7 _____ a piece of land on a farm

8 _____ cows

9 _____ a grass crop, grown to make flour for bread

10 _____ a piece of land for growing grapes for wine

11 _____ animal waste used for fertilizer

12 _____ a farm building often used for storing crops

Think about

1 Have you ever visited a farm? When? Where? What did you do? What did you see?

2 Are farmers usually rich or poor in your country? What do they usually grow?

3 Would you like to be a farmer? Why? Why not?

3.3 Tools and their uses

Words in context *Read the following passages and do the exercises.*

Imagine that you have two pieces of wood and some tools in your hands. How many different ways of joining them together can you think of? Before you read any further, spend a few moments trying to answer this question. *There are, in fact, many possible ways. Here are six.*

I The simplest method of all is probably to take some **string** and **tie** one piece of wood to the other. This method will probably not keep the two pieces together for very long.

2 Another simple way is to take some wood **glue** and put it on both pieces of wood. You will have to press the two pieces together very hard and if you are lucky your two pieces will **stick** together.

3 Another way is to use **nails**. You'll need a **hammer**. Then bang the nails into the wood. The nails must not be too big or they will crack the wood. And they must not be too small or the wood will not stay together.

4 If you want to use **screws** to put two pieces of wood together, you first have to **drill** a hole through one of the pieces. You also have to start a hole in the second piece of wood. Then push the screw through the first hole and use a **screwdriver** to **screw** it in until it is tightly in the second piece of wood. Using screws is usually a very strong way of joining two pieces of wood.

5 Instead of using screws you could use a **nut** and **bolt**. This time you have to drill a hole through both pieces of wood. Then you push the bolt through both holes and **tighten** a nut onto the end of the bolt using a **spanner**.

6 The most complicated way of joining two pieces of wood together is to make a joint. To do this you need a **saw**. There are many different types of joints, but the basic idea is to cut a shape in one piece of wood and to **saw** out a matching piece in the other piece of wood. Then you fit the two pieces together and stick them with glue.

Exercise 1

Match the six different ways of joining wood together, described above (1–6), with the pictures below.

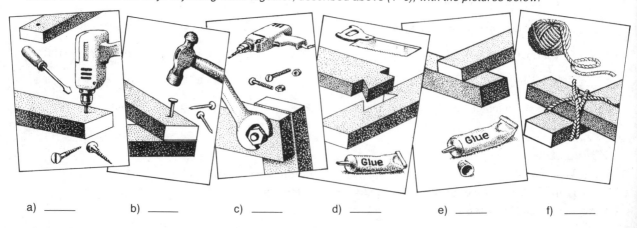

a) _____ b) _____ c) _____ d) _____ e) _____ f) _____

Exercise 2

Divide the following words into two groups: tools and things that are used with tools.

| screw | hammer | nail | glue | spanner | saw | bolt | screwdriver |

tools   **things used with tools**

_____   _____

_____   _____

_____   _____

_____   _____

Exercise 3

Complete the first half of the sentence on the left with the best phrase from the right.

1 She drilled _____   a) the piece of wood in two.

2 She sawed _____   b) the pieces of wood together with string.

3 She tightened _____   c) a nail.

4 She stuck _____   d) a hole in the piece of wood.

5 She tied _____   e) the pieces of wood together with glue.

6 She banged in _____   f) the screw with a screwdriver.

Just for fun

The words on the right are hidden in the word square. Can you find them? If you do not know all the words, look them up in your dictionary.

K	P	S	R	E	I	L	P	O	P
S	N	R	C	F	I	N	K	I	R
N	A	I	L	R	I	F	H	K	I
A	R	W	A	R	E	S	A	N	L
D	E	O	D	E	C	W	M	H	L
E	N	D	D	E	M	K	A	I	L
P	A	A	E	G	N	M	I	D	I
S	P	E	R	I	M	M	L	R	R
S	I	R	F	E	E	X	I	E	D
W	R	E	R	I	W	E	R	S	C

saw
spade
pliers
hammer
screw
nail
ladder
wire
knife
drill

Think about

1 What advice would you give someone on how to use a hammer, a saw and a screwdriver?

2 Have you ever made anything with tools? What did you make? What tools did you use?

3 Do schools teach both boys and girls how to use tools in your country?

4 What are the basic tools that should be in every home?

3.4 Shopping

Words in context *Read the story and do the exercises.*

Exercise 1

Decide if the following statements are true (T) or false (F) according to the story.

1 _____ The man returned the television because it was broken.

2 _____ The man wanted a refund.

3 _____ The salesman offered him a credit note.

4 _____ Every television in the store was reduced.

5 _____ The Zandy 3000 was being sold at half price.

6 _____ If the Zandy 3000 breaks in the next year, the man will get his money back.

7 _____ The Zandy 3000 cost more than the television that the man had returned.

8 _____ The man paid by cheque.

9 _____ The man bought the last Zandy 3000 in the store.

10 _____ The salesman was very good at his job.

Exercise 2

Decide if the following sentences are similar (S) or different (D) in meaning.

1 It's fifty per cent off. _____ It's half price.

2 It's a bargain. _____ It's a good deal.

3 It's reduced. _____ It's at the normal price.

4 It's at the retail price. _____ It's at the wholesale price.

5 It's a big discount. _____ It's a great reduction.

6 It's in a sale. _____ It's at the normal retail price.

Exercise 3

Match the words with their definitions.

```
a) refund        c) exchange   e) receipt      g) credit card
b) credit note   d) guarantee  f) cheque
```

1 _____ a piece of paper that says that you bought something in a store

2 _____ money that you get back after you return goods to a store

3 _____ a piece of paper promising you money, a replacement or repair if
something goes wrong with what you have bought

4 _____ a piece of plastic that you can use like money to pay for goods

5 _____ a piece of paper that says you can spend money in that store.

6 _____ goods in return for goods that you bought in a store

7 _____ a piece of paper that says that you will pay with money in your bank

Dictionary work

Each of the words in the box is a type of shop. Match the shops with examples of what
they sell. Do as many as you can and then check your answers in a dictionary.

```
a) stationer's      c) greengrocer's e) department store g) off-licence   i) supermarket k) jeweller's
b) hardware store   d) chemist's     f) baker's          h) newsagent's j) florist's     l) boutique
```

1 _____ alcoholic drinks

2 _____ flowers

3 _____ everything

4 _____ fruit and vegetables

5 _____ rings and necklaces

6 _____ all kinds of food

7 _____ paper

8 _____ newspapers, cigarettes

9 _____ fashionable clothes

10 _____ bread and cakes

11 _____ tools

12 _____ medicines

Think about

1 Do most shops in your country give refunds or credit notes to dissatisfied customers?

2 When are the biggest sales in the shops in your country? Can you get good bargains?

3 Do people usually shop in big department stores and supermarkets, or small shops?
Which do you prefer and why?

3.5 Money

Words in context *Read the story and do the exercises.*

René Labouche was a young man with very little money, but very big dreams. He worked in a factory and **earned** only a few hundred francs a month. He **owned** almost nothing – some old furniture, some clothes and an old bicycle, but he dreamed of having a big house and a big car.

Every day René **purchased** five lottery tickets for five francs each. He dreamed that one day he would win the big prize in the national lottery and become a millionaire. Then he could **afford** to buy whatever he wanted and would never have to work another day in his life.

One day as usual René opened the newspaper to check his numbers. He read the numbers slowly, '6 – 11 – 31 – 32 – 47 – 49.' Those were his numbers! He looked again. '6 – 11 – 31 – 32 – 47 – 49.' He had won. He had won the national lottery. He was a millionaire!

Suddenly everyone wanted to be René's friend. Many people came to him and asked if they could **borrow** money. 'Of course, we'll **pay back** every centime,' they said. Others told him about their wonderful ideas for **making money**. 'If you **invest** 500,000 francs in this project,' they said, 'I promise in two years you will **make a** big **profit** and double your money.'

The money had come easily and René **spent** it easily. He **lent** 25,000 francs to this friend and 50,000 francs to that. He invested 500,000 francs here and 800,000 francs there. He made no effort to **save** anything.

When he bought something he never looked at the price. If something **cost** a thousand francs, he paid a thousand francs. He never worried about whether it was **worth** it or not. He bought cars, jewellery, and clothes. He also bought airline tickets. He flew first class to all the major cities of the world. He stayed at the best hotels, he ate at the best restaurants, and he bought the finest clothes.

Then one day, when he went to pay his bill at a hotel in Rio, the manager had to tell him, 'I'm sorry sir, but I'm afraid your credit card company will not pay this bill.'

René flew home. It was true he had no more money. He went back to the people who **owed** him money, but they were unable to **repay** him. The projects in which he had invested his money had all **made losses**. In six months René had spent ten million francs.

René now had no choice. He had to sell the cars, the watches and the clothes and he had to go back to work in the factory.

Exercise 1

Find the correct ending for each sentence according to the information in the story.

1 _____ René used to earn		a) a lot of money from him.
2 _____ René used to purchase		b) him a lot of money.
3 _____ René used to own		c) ten million francs.
4 _____ René won		d) money in some of his friends' ideas.
5 _____ René's friends borrowed		e) a few hundred francs a month.
6 _____ René invested		f) the money he had lent them.
7 _____ René's friends owed		g) lottery tickets every day.
8 _____ René's friends couldn't repay		h) an old bike and some old furniture.

Exercise 2

Decide which phrase correctly finishes each sentence.

1 If I lend you money
    a) you owe me money.
    b) I owe you money.

2 If I borrow money from you
    a) you should pay me back.
    b) I should repay you.

3 If you can't afford things
    a) you can borrow money from me.
    b) you can lend me money.

4 If I sell something for more than I paid for it
    a) I have made a loss.
    b) I have made a profit.

5 If I purchase something and pay more than it's worth
    a) I will probably make a loss when I sell it.
    b) I will probably make a profit when I sell it.

Exercise 3

Fill each blank with one of the words listed below.

spend	lend	cost	worth	afford
own	earn	sell	invest	save

In Britain and the United States, many people would like to _____ their own homes, but it is usually very

difficult to _____ enough money. Most people _____ as much as they _____

each month. But if you can't _____ to buy a house, often you can get a bank to _____ you

the money to buy one. The bank knows that a house is a very good place for you to _____ your money.

A few years after you buy it, a house is usually _____ much more than it originally _____

you, so you can _____ it for a big profit.

Dictionary work

Match the words with their definitions. Do as many as you can and then check your answers in the dictionary.

> a) fees b) interest c) taxes d) wages e) salary f) rent g) pension h) fare i) cash j) change

1 _____ money paid for a place to live

2 _____ money paid to the government

3 _____ money paid for professional services

4 _____ money in coins and notes, not cheques

5 _____ money paid to workers by the hour or week

6 _____ money paid as charges on the money you borrow

7 _____ money paid to workers for a month's or year's work

8 _____ money paid to older people who no longer work

9 _____ money returned to you after you pay too much

10 _____ money paid for a journey by bus, train or plane

Think about

1 Where does the money go? What percentage of your money do you spend on food, transport, housing, taxes, clothes and entertainment?

2 One of Shakespeare's characters says, 'Neither a borrower, nor a lender be.'' What does it mean? Do you agree?

3 How easy is it for a poor man to become rich in your country?

Vocabulary review

3 At work (Units 3.1–3.5)

3.1 Jobs

blue-collar
boss
businessman/woman
career
doctor
job
manager
nurse
office worker
out of work
profession
retire
sales representative
salesperson
secretary
skilled
teacher
unemployed
unskilled
white-collar

3.2 Farm work

axe
barn
bull
cattle
chop
crops
feed
fertilize
field
gather
harvest
hen
manure
pick
plant
plough
reap
shepherd
soil
spray
store
tractor
vineyard
water *v*
wheat

3.3 Tools and their uses

bolt
drill
glue
hammer
knife
ladder
nail
nut
pliers
saw
screw
screwdriver
spade
spanner (*AmE* wrench)
stick
string
tie
tighten
wire

3.4 Shopping

baker's
bargain
boutique
cheap
chemist's (*AmE* pharmacy)
cheque
credit card
credit note
deal
department store
discount
exchange
expensive
florist's
greengrocer's
guarantee
hardware store
jeweller's
low price
newsagent's
off: £2 off
off-licence (*AmE* liquor store)
receipt
reduced
reduction
refund
retail price
sale
stationer's
supermarket
wholesale price

3.5 Money

afford
borrow
cash
change
cost
earn
fare
fees
interest
invest
lend
loss
    make a loss
money
    make money
owe
own
pay back
pension
profit
    make a profit
purchase
rent
repay
salary
save
spend
tax
wages
worth
    be worth

Test yourself 5

Use the words from the **Vocabulary review** to help you fill in the blanks in these sentences. The number of dashes corresponds to the number of letters in the missing word. More than one answer may be possible, but there is always one best answer.

1 I could never _ _ _ _ _ _ a Rolls Royce. They're much too expensive.

2 The busiest time of the year on a farm is always _ _ _ _ _ _ _ time.

3 Teaching is usually a very poorly-paid _ _ _ _ _ _ _ _ _ _ _ .

4 Many _ _ _ _ _ _ _ _ _ _ workers are losing their jobs because robots and computers are doing their work.

5 Some famous _ _ _ _ _ _ _ _ _ _ _ stores are Harrods, Galeries Lafayette and Macy's.

6 We don't have to work so hard when the _ _ _ _ _ isn't in the office.

7 I haven't got enough cash on me. Is it all right if I pay by _ _ _ _ _ _ _ _ ?

8 She is a very rich woman. She keeps horses and _ _ _ _ _ _ _ on her land in Florida.

9 Because I work for a clothes shop, I can get a 20 per cent _ _ _ _ _ _ _ _ on any clothes I buy.

10 Have you seen the _ _ _ _ _ _ _ _ _ _ _ _ ? I need it to tighten these screws.

11 George was the best _ _ _ _ _ _ _ _ _ _ _ _ in the shop last year. He sold three thousand pairs of shoes.

12 Be careful while you are cutting the wood. This _ _ _ _ is very sharp.

13 This year I have _ _ _ _ _ _ _ _ some tomatoes in my garden. I hope they grow.

14 I bought this stereo for £60. I think that was a real _ _ _ _ _ _ _ .

15 In many countries the government takes money in _ _ _ _ _ _ out of people's pay.

16 Pass me the hammer and some _ _ _ _ _ _ , and I'll mend this broken chair.

17 The farmer taught his son how to drive the _ _ _ _ _ _ _ across the fields.

18 I haven't got enough money on me. Could you _ _ _ _ _ me some till tomorrow?

19 You can probably mend that broken cup with some good _ _ _ _ _ .

20 In some countries, when you're _ _ _ _ _ _ _ _ _ _ _ , the government will give you money to live on until you find a job.

21 You'll need a longer _ _ _ _ _ _ _ to reach those windows. They're very high.

22 In which month do the farmers _ _ _ _ _ their grapes in the South of France?

23 If you want to return anything to that shop, you'll have to show your _ _ _ _ _ _ _ .

24 You borrowed £100 from me last year. Now you _ _ _ _ me £120,

25 because I am charging you 20 per cent _ _ _ _ _ _ _ _ _ .

3.6 Education

This is a conversation between Tom, a **pupil** at a **secondary school** and an old friend, Mark, who has just started at **university**.

Words in context

Read the dialogue and do the exercises.

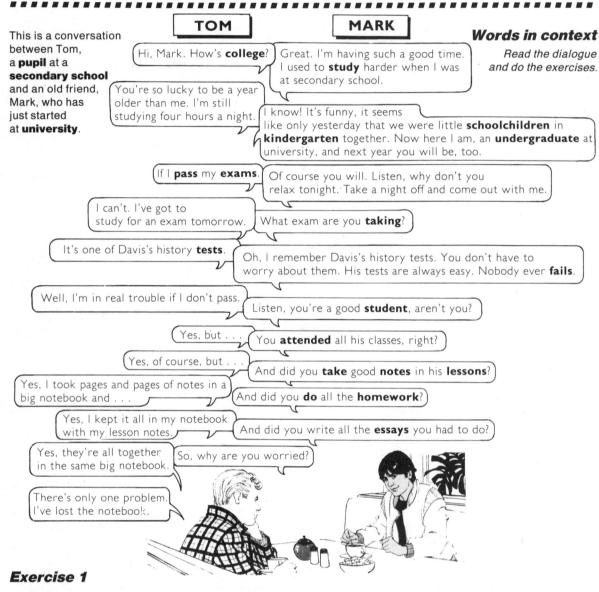

TOM

MARK

Hi, Mark. How's **college**?

Great. I'm having such a good time. I used to **study** harder when I was at secondary school.

You're so lucky to be a year older than me. I'm still studying four hours a night.

I know! It's funny, it seems like only yesterday that we were little **schoolchildren** in **kindergarten** together. Now here I am, an **undergraduate** at university, and next year you will be, too.

If I **pass** my **exams**.

Of course you will. Listen, why don't you relax tonight. Take a night off and come out with me.

I can't. I've got to study for an exam tomorrow.

What exam are you **taking**?

It's one of Davis's history **tests**.

Oh, I remember Davis's history tests. You don't have to worry about them. His tests are always easy. Nobody ever **fails**.

Well, I'm in real trouble if I don't pass.

Listen, you're a good **student**, aren't you?

Yes, but . . .

You **attended** all his classes, right?

Yes, of course, but . . .

And did you **take** good **notes** in his **lessons**?

Yes, I took pages and pages of notes in a big notebook and . . .

And did you **do** all the **homework**?

Yes, I kept it all in my notebook with my lesson notes.

And did you write all the **essays** you had to do?

Yes, they're all together in the same big notebook.

So, why are you worried?

There's only one problem. I've lost the notebook.

Exercise 1

Choose the best answers according to the information in the dialogue.

1 Who is probably older?
   a) Tom   b) Mark   c) impossible to know

2 How many years have Tom and Mark known each other?
   a) about four   b) about eight
   c) about twelve

3 Who now does more studying?
   a) Tom   b) Mark   c) they do the same

4 Has Mark ever taken Davis's history test?
   a) yes   b) no   c) impossible to know

5 Is Tom a good student?
   a) yes   b) no   c) impossible to know

6 Is Tom going to fail his history test?
   a) yes   b) no   c) impossible to know

Exercise 2

Put the following words into one of the three columns.

| undergraduate | essay | homework | college | kindergarten | pupil | student | notes | university |

place for learning	person who studies	something produced by a student
_____	_____	_____
_____	_____	_____
_____	_____	_____

Exercise 3

Put the following events in order of which happens first, second and third.

1	___ ___ ___	a) take an exam	b) pass an exam	c) study for an exam
2	___ ___ ___	a) go to college	b) go to secondary school	c) go to kindergarten
3	___ ___ ___	a) learn	b) listen	c) forget
4	___ ___ ___	a) be a teacher	b) be a schoolchild	c) be an undergraduate
5	___ ___ ___	a) have a lesson	b) do homework	c) take a test

Just for fun

Which of the following characteristics do you like best in a teacher? Put them in order from 1–8.

is friendly _____

gives frequent tests _____

has a good sense of humour _____

makes a subject interesting _____

gives a lot of homework _____

is young and attractive _____

keeps good control of the students' behaviour _____

knows his or her subject well _____

Discuss your answers with someone else.

Think about

1 At what ages do you take important examinations in your country?
2 Describe the education system in your country.
3 What subjects do you think are the most important to study at school?
4 Do you think a good education should prepare you for life in general or for a particular job?

3.7 Medical matters

■■■

Doctor Lennox is a radio doctor. She answers listeners' questions about their medical problems. Read their questions to her.

Words in context

Read the passages and do the exercises.

a)  Hello, Doctor Lennox. Well, three days ago I fell over and cut my arm. There was a little blood, but it soon stopped **bleeding** and I forgot about it. Now the **wound** is painful and red. It **hurts** when I touch it. I also think I may have a **temperature**. I feel a little hot and quite weak. Do you think I should see my doctor?

b) 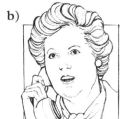 Doctor Lennox, I am a 63-year-old woman. A few months ago, I was walking upstairs when I suddenly became very **faint** and almost fell over. Now, whenever I do just a little exercise I get **out of breath** very quickly. Even when I'm sleeping I have breathing problems. I wake up in the middle of the night and can't get back to sleep. I'm really worried, because I have never had **insomnia** in my life before. I don't have a **pain** in my chest, so I don't think I have heart problems. I'm very worried. What do you think?

c)  For the last two days, Doctor Lennox, I have been feeling absolutely terrible. My whole body **aches**. I have a **backache** and all my muscles ache. I have a terrible **headache** too. But the worst thing is the **vomiting**. Food just won't stay in my stomach for more than a few minutes. And the **diarrhea** – I'm in the bathroom every half an hour. I telephoned my doctor and asked for a **prescription** for some medicine, but she said there wasn't much she could do for me. She said I should stay in bed and drink a lot. Is that right?

d)  I hope you can understand me all right, doctor, but I can't talk very well because of my **sore throat**. I've had it a few months now. And a **cough**, too, even though I don't smoke. And I seem to be tired all the time, but I'm never so ill that I can't go to work. I've been to the doctor and had some tests, but they can't find anything wrong with me. What do you think I should do now?

Exercise 1

Here are Doctor Lennox's answers. Match her answers to the questions.

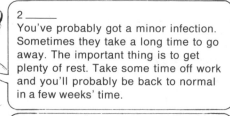

1 _____
You should see a doctor as soon as possible. Your doctor will arrange for you to have a complete series of tests. I'm afraid you really could be very seriously ill, you know.

2 _____
You've probably got a minor infection. Sometimes they take a long time to go away. The important thing is to get plenty of rest. Take some time off work and you'll probably be back to normal in a few weeks' time.

3 _____
It sounds as if you have got an infection. You'll have to see your doctor, who will probably write you a prescription for an antibiotic and some medicine to put on your skin as well.

4 _____
You have what is commonly called stomach flu. It's most important that you drink a lot. You should feel better soon, but if it continues much longer you should see your doctor.

Exercise 2

Complete the first half of each sentence with the best second half.

1 If you have a temperature   _____   a) you get some pain and redness.

2 If you feel faint   _____   b) you have difficulty sleeping.

3 If you have insomnia   _____   c) you feel hot.

4 If you have a sore throat   _____   d) your chest may hurt.

5 If you have a bad cough   _____   e) the contents of your stomach come out of your mouth.

6 If you have an infected wound   _____   f) you have difficulty talking and swallowing.

7 If you vomit   _____   g) you have difficulty standing up.

Exercise 3

Read the sentences. Then decide who is most likely to be saying them.

a) 'My fingers hurt.'	d) 'My knees are killing me.'
b) 'I have a terrible pain in my chest.'	e) 'I have such a terrible headache.'
c) 'I've got a dreadful stomachache.'	f) 'My shoulder is aching terribly.'

1 _____ Someone who had to sit for four hours in a plane near a noisy engine.

2 _____ Someone who has just bicycled 100 miles.

3 _____ Someone who has eaten some food which was not fresh.

4 _____ Someone who tried to lift something that was too heavy for him.

5 _____ Someone who closed a door on her hand.

6 _____ Someone who is having a heart attack.

Just for fun

If someone told you that they had one of the following medical problems, what would you tell them to do to help them get better quickly?

1 a headache   5 a burn on the finger
2 a sore throat   6 a bleeding nose
3 a cough   7 insomnia
4 diarrhea   8 sore muscles after exercise

Discuss your answers with someone else.

Think about

1 Is it expensive to visit the doctor in your country?
2 If you could be a doctor which type would you be and why?
3 What are the most common symptoms (signs) of flu?
4 What are the most common illnesses in your country? What are their symptoms?

3.8 The law

JURY FINDS MULLINS GUILTY

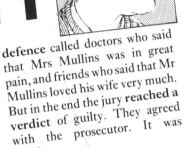

A **jury** of seven men and five women said today that 78-year-old Mr. Andrew Mullins was **guilty** of murdering his 80-year-old wife, Edith. Six weeks ago, Mullins **went on trial** for murder.

During the trial Mullins said that he had killed his wife because she was very ill and had lost her mind. He said, 'The woman I killed was not my wife. It was a body in pain and a mind with no memory.'

He **committed the crime** on the night of August 10th in their home in the small town of Palmston Beach. That morning his wife had looked at him with empty eyes and asked, 'Who are you?' That evening she was in terrible pain and kept saying, 'Help me, help me.' So as she slept on the sofa that night, Mullins put a gun against her head and shot her. Then he telephoned the police and told them what he had done. The police came to the house and **arrested** him. Two days later he was **charged** with murder.

During the six-week trial, there were many **witnesses** who **gave evidence**. The **prosecution** called witnesses who said that Mrs Mullins liked to go out, that she smiled and wore make-up. The **defence** called doctors who said that Mrs Mullins was in great pain, and friends who said that Mr Mullins loved his wife very much. But in the end the jury **reached a verdict** of guilty. They agreed with the prosecutor. It was murder.

Tomorrow the **judge** will **pass sentence**. The law says that he must **send** Mullins **to prison** for at least twenty-five years. That means he will not **be released** from prison until he is 103 years old!

There are many people in Palmston Beach tonight who think the law is wrong. Mullins is not a **criminal**. He is not a dangerous man. Perhaps he is just a man who loved his wife too much.

Exercise 1

Ask the questions to the following answers.

1 78. _____

2 Six weeks ago. _____

3 He shot her. _____

4 Acquaintances, doctors and friends.

_____

5 At least twenty-five years.

_____

6 When he is 103 years old.

_____

> **?** Do you think Mullins should go to prison?

72

Exercise 2

Match the people on the left with what they do during a trial.

1 The judge	_____	a) gives evidence.
2 A witness	_____	b) reaches a verdict of innocent or guilty.
3 The jury	_____	c) tries to show the person on trial is guilty.
4 The prosecution	_____	d) controls the trial and passes sentence.

Exercise 3

Put the following events in the story of Charles Mercer in the order in which they are most likely to have happened.

1 First, _____		a) the jury reached a verdict.
2 Later _____		b) he was arrested by the police.
3 Next, _____		c) the jury considered the evidence.
4 So then _____		d) he was sent to prison.
5 Now _____		e) Charles Mercer committed a crime.
6 And _____		f) the police charged him.
7 Then _____		g) he was released from prison.
8 Then _____		h) the judge passed sentence.
9 After that _____		i) he went on trial.
10 So _____		j) the prosecution called witnesses.
11 A few years later _____	·	k) the defence said that he was not a criminal.

Dictionary work

Match the names of different crimes to examples of those crimes. Do as many as you can and then check your answers in the dictionary.

a) hijacking	c) burglary	e) kidnapping	g) blackmail
b) shoplifting	d) rape	f) drug-dealing	h) smuggling

1 _____ taking a child away from his or her family

2 _____ not paying taxes on goods from another country

3 _____ getting money by promising not to tell a secret

4 _____ selling cocaine

5 _____ forcing somebody to have sex

6 _____ taking control of an aeroplane by force

7 _____ taking goods from a shop without paying

8 _____ going into a house and stealing

Think about

1 What are the most common crimes in your country?
2 Do you think crime has increased in the last twenty-five years? If you do, what do you think are the reasons?
3 What do you think is the best way to fight crime?

3.9 Politics

Words in context

Read the passage and do the exercises.

How can you become the leader of a country?

One way is to be born into the **royal family**. If you are a **prince**, especially the eldest son, then one day you can become **king**. And in some countries, if you are the eldest daughter (a **princess**) and there are no sons, then one day you could become **queen**. Of course, today there are not many royal families, and those that still exist do not usually have the power to make laws and **govern**. A more usual way to become leader of your country, however, is to become a **politician** and then to become the leader of the most popular **political party**. In most countries where the people **elect** their **government**, the **voters** usually **vote** for a person who belongs to one of the main political parties. This person is usually the **candidate** for the local region. The candidate who receives the most **votes** becomes the political representative for that region and takes a seat (a place) in the national **parliament** or **assembly**. The political party which wins the most seats then has the right to form a government and take power. The head of that political party then becomes the **president** (in countries such as Taiwan or Italy) or the **prime minister** (in countries such as Great Britain and Japan).

In some countries, such as France and the United States, the system is a little different. Every seven years in France, and every four years in the United States, there are presidential **elections**. At this time the people vote directly for the person that they want to become president. Regional elections are independent from presidential elections. This means that it is possible to become the President and yet not be the leader of the most popular political party.

Exercise 1

Choose the best answer.

1 In a royal family where there are three sons and three daughters, the next king or queen is most likely to be
   a) the eldest son   b) the eldest daughter
   c) the eldest child

2 In most electoral systems, the regional candidate who gets the most votes
   a) does not usually belong to a political party
   b) will represent that region in the national parliament
   c) will form a government and take power

3 In a country such as Great Britain, the political leader
   a) belongs to the royal family
   b) is called the president
   c) belongs to the most popular political party

4 In the United States, the person who becomes President
   a) always belongs to the most popular political party
   b) changes every four years
   c) is elected directly by the people

Exercise 2

Match the people on the left with the best definitions on the right.

1 _____ king   a) female relative of a royal family

2 _____ president   b) the head of government in Japan

3 _____ queen   c) someone who chooses a political representative

4 _____ princess   d) male head of a royal family

5 _____ voter   e) female head of a royal family

6 _____ candidate   f) the head of government in the United States

7 _____ prime minister g) male relative of a royal family

8 _____ prince   h) someone who tries to win a place in the national assembly

Exercise 3

Underline the correct word in the following sentences and decide whether the word is a
noun (N), a verb (V) or an adjective (A).

1 _____ Are you interested in (politics/political)?

2 _____ In many countries under 50 per cent of the people actually (vote/voter) in an election.

3 _____ The people who (govern/government) the country are called the

4 _____ (govern/government).

5 _____ In France they (elect/election) a new leader every seven years

6 _____ in a (presidential/president)

7 _____ (elect/election).

8 _____ He is the most important (political/politician) in his

9 _____ (political/politician) party.

Dictionary work

Each word in English which has two or more syllables has a strong stress or emphasis
on one of the syllables. Underline the strong-stressed syllable as in the example. Do you know what
the words mean? Do as many as you can and then check the answers in your dictionary.

Example: election

1 republic	4 president	7 conservative	10 ambassador	13 politics
2 political	5 politician	8 democracy	11 democratic	14 industry
3 industrial	6 society	9 social	12 economy	15 economic

Think about

1 Can you describe how a person becomes the political leader of your country?

2 Which countries have royal families? Do these royal families have much political power?

3 Do you have political parties in your country? What are the differences between them?

3.10 Space

Words in context *Read the passage and do the exercises.*

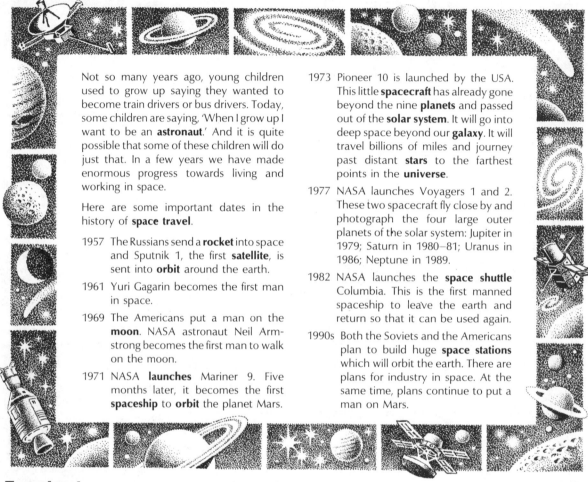

Not so many years ago, young children used to grow up saying they wanted to become train drivers or bus drivers. Today, some children are saying, 'When I grow up I want to be an **astronaut**.' And it is quite possible that some of these children will do just that. In a few years we have made enormous progress towards living and working in space.

Here are some important dates in the history of **space travel**.

1957 The Russians send a **rocket** into space and Sputnik 1, the first **satellite**, is sent into **orbit** around the earth.

1961 Yuri Gagarin becomes the first man in space.

1969 The Americans put a man on the **moon**. NASA astronaut Neil Armstrong becomes the first man to walk on the moon.

1971 NASA **launches** Mariner 9. Five months later, it becomes the first **spaceship** to **orbit** the planet Mars.

1973 Pioneer 10 is launched by the USA. This little **spacecraft** has already gone beyond the nine **planets** and passed out of the **solar system**. It will go into deep space beyond our **galaxy**. It will travel billions of miles and journey past distant **stars** to the farthest points in the **universe**.

1977 NASA launches Voyagers 1 and 2. These two spacecraft fly close by and photograph the four large outer planets of the solar system: Jupiter in 1979; Saturn in 1980–81; Uranus in 1986; Neptune in 1989.

1982 NASA launches the **space shuttle** Columbia. This is the first manned spaceship to leave the earth and return so that it can be used again.

1990s Both the Soviets and the Americans plan to build huge **space stations** which will orbit the earth. There are plans for industry in space. At the same time, plans continue to put a man on Mars.

Exercise 1

Decide if the following statements are true (T) or false (F) according to the information in the passage.

1 _____ The Russians sent a man into space in 1957.

2 _____ American astronauts landed on the moon in 1969.

3 _____ Mariner 9 landed on Mars in 1971.

4 _____ It took nine years for Voyager 2 to reach Uranus.

5 _____ Pioneer 10 is still travelling in space.

6 _____ A space shuttle has been orbiting the earth since 1982.

7 _____ In the 1990s there are plans to put a space station into orbit around Mars.

Exercise 2

Fill in the blank with the correct missing word or words, so that each pair of items in column B has the same relationship as each pair in column A.

A		**B**
1 pilot	: plane	_____ : spaceship
2 take off	: plane	_____ : rocket
3 flight path	: plane	_____ : satellite

Exercise 3

Put the following into order from smallest (1) to largest (8).

a) galaxy   b) satellite   c) universe   d) planet   e) moon   f) solar system   g) star   h) space shuttle

1 ____   2 ____   3 ____   4 ____   5 ____   6 ____   7 ____   8 ____

Just for fun

Do you know the position of the planets in our solar system? See if you can name the planets on the diagram below.

a) Earth   b) Jupiter   c) Venus   d) Saturn   e) Mercury   f) Mars   g) Uranus   h) Pluto   i) Neptune

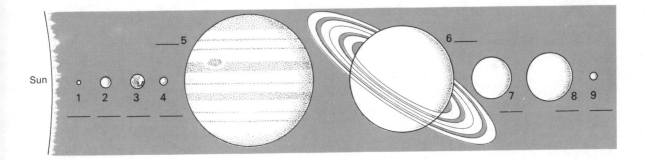

Think about

1 Do you think space exploration is important?
2 Has your country been involved in space exploration in any way?
3 Do you think that in the future many people will travel to other planets and live in spaceships? Would you like to?
4 Is there life on other planets?

Vocabulary review

3 At work (Units 3.6–3.10)

3.6 Education

attend class
college
homework
  do homework
essay
exam
fail a test/an exam
kindergarten
lecture
lesson
notes
  take notes
pass a test/an exam
pupil
schoolchild, schoolchildren
secondary school
student
study
take a test/an exam
test
undergraduate
university

3.7 Medical matters

ache
backache
bleed
cough
diarrhea
faint
headache
hurt
insomnia
out of breath
pain
prescription
temperature
  have a temperature
throat
  sore throat
vomit
wound

3.8 The law

arrest
blackmail
burglary
charge v
crime
  commit a crime
criminal
defence
drug-dealing
evidence
  give evidence
go on trial
guilty
hijacking
judge
jury
kidnapping
police
prison
prosecutor
rape
release from prison
send to prison
sentence
  pass sentence
shoplifting
smuggling
trial
verdict
  reach a verdict
witness

3.9 Politics

ambassador
assembly
candidate
conservative
democracy
democratic
economic
economy
elect
election
govern
government
industrial
industry

king
parliament
political
political party
politician
politics
president
prime minister
prince
princess
queen
republic
royal family
social
society
vote
voter

3.10 Space

astronaut
galaxy
launch
moon
orbit
planet
rocket
satellite
send into orbit
solar system
spacecraft
spaceship
space shuttle
space station
space travel
star
universe

Test yourself 6

Use the words from the **Vocabulary review** to help you fill in the blanks in these sentences. The number of dashes corresponds to the number of letters in the missing word have been given to help you. More than one answer may be possible, but there is always one best answer.

1 Before the Americans sent an ＿＿＿＿＿＿＿＿＿＿ into space, they sent a dog.

2 The exam seemed terribly difficult. I think I must have ＿＿＿＿＿＿ .

3 In the last general election, what percentage of the population ＿＿＿＿＿ ?

4 Which is the nearest ＿＿＿＿＿＿＿ to the Earth?

5 Would you go to work if you had a ＿＿＿＿＿＿＿＿＿＿＿ of 38°C?

6 Whenever I sit in the smoking section of an aeroplane, I get a terrible ＿＿＿＿＿＿＿＿ .

7 The judge sentenced the two men to twenty years in ＿＿＿＿＿＿ .

8 They were found guilty of ＿＿＿＿＿＿＿＿＿＿ . They had taken the young son of the prime minister and demanded £20 million.

9 In 1986 the space ＿＿＿＿＿＿＿ , Challenger, exploded after take-off, killing all seven astronauts.

10 The professor asked the students what they were going to do when they had finished at the ＿＿＿＿＿＿＿＿ .

11 There is one side of the ＿＿＿＿＿ which can never be seen from the Earth.

12 There is a great deal of international interest in the British royal family, especially in the princes and ＿＿＿＿＿＿＿＿＿＿ .

13 When the teacher asked for last night's ＿＿＿＿＿＿＿＿ , Miriam said she hadn't done it.

14 People who smoke often have a bad ＿＿＿＿＿＿ .

15 There were six people who said they had seen the crime, but each ＿＿＿＿＿＿＿＿ said they had seen something different.

16 A political system where the people vote for the government is usually called a ＿＿＿＿＿＿＿＿＿ .

17 The political and ＿＿＿＿＿＿＿＿ systems of the United States and the Soviet Union are very different.

18 One of the first signs of a heart attack is a sharp ＿＿＿＿＿ in the left arm.

19 Most ＿＿＿＿＿＿＿＿＿＿＿＿＿ find that their most difficult year at university is their final year of study.

20 After I have my teeth cleaned at the dentist's, they ＿＿＿＿＿ for a day or two.

21 The police ＿＿＿＿＿＿＿＿＿ him after finding his fingerprints on the gun.

22 There are a great many telecommunications ＿＿＿＿＿＿＿＿＿＿ orbiting the Earth.

23 At what age do you have to ＿＿＿＿＿ important exams in your country?

24 In Japan the head of the ＿＿＿＿＿＿＿＿＿＿＿ is called the Prime Minister.

25 The jury listened to a great deal of evidence during a very long ＿＿＿＿＿＿ .

British English and American English differences

■■■

The words in the left-hand column are British English (*BrE*) words which are used in the *Vocabulary Builders*. These words are different in American English. Some of the differences are in spelling only. The words in the right-hand column show the usual American English (*AmE*) equivalent.

BrE	*AmE*
athletics	track and field
autumn	fall
bath	bathtub
behaviour	behavior
biscuit	cookie
cancelled	canceled
centre	center
chemist's	pharmacy
colour	color
coloured	colored
cushion	pillow
defence	defense
do the washing-up/do the dishes	do the dishes
favourite	favorite
film	movie
football	soccer
go to the cinema	go to the movies
grey	gray
have a bath/shower	take a bath/shower
hockey	field hockey
humour	humor
labourer	laborer
metre	meter
neighbour	neighbor
off-licence	liquor store
practise *v*	practice
programme	program
pyjamas	pajamas
shop	store
spanner	wrench
storey	story
tap	faucet
theatre	theater
tin/can	can
tinned/canned	canned
travelled	traveled
trousers	pants

British English and American English differences are also shown on the **Vocabulary review** pages.

Answers to the riddles in Unit 2.5

1 table   2 umbrella   3 tomorrow

Index

dining room/'daɪnɪŋ ruːm/ 1.1
dining table/'daɪnɪŋ ˌteɪbəl/ 1.2
dinner/'dɪnər/ 2.4
dirty/'dɜːti/ 1.5
disc jockey/'dɪsk ˌdʒɒki/ 2.4
disco/'dɪskəʊ/ 2.4
discount/'dɪskaʊnt/ 3.4
discuss/dɪ'skʌs/ 2.10
dishwasher/'dɪʃˌwɒʃər/ 1.5
dive/daɪv/ 2.2
doctor/'dɒktər/ 3.1
documentary
ˌ/ˌdɒkjʊ'mentəri/ 2.8
do homework/duː
'həʊmwɜːk/ 3.6
do the washing up/duː ðə
ˌwɒʃɪŋ 'ʌp/ 1.5
downstairs/ˌdaʊn'steəz/ 1.1
drawer/drɔːr/ 1.2
dream n/driːm/ 1.3
dress/dres/ 1.9
dried/draɪd/ 1.8
drill/drɪl/ 3.3
drink/drɪŋk/ 1.7
drowsy/'draʊzi/ 1.3
drug-dealing/'drʌg ˌdiːlɪŋ/ 3.8
drums/drʌmz/ 2.7
dry yourself/'draɪ jəself/ 1.4
dust/dʌst/ 1.5
earn/ɜːn/ 3.5
eat/iːt/ 1.7
economic/ˌekə'nɒmɪk/ 3.9
economy/ɪ'kɒnəmi/ 3.9
editorial/ˌedɪ'tɔːriəl/ 2.9
elect/ɪ'lekt/ 3.9
election/ɪ'lekʃən/ 3.9
encyclopedia
/ɪnˌsaɪklə'piːdiə/ 2.9
enjoy yourself/ɪn'dʒɔɪ
jəself/ 2.3
entertainer/ˌentə'teɪnər/ 2.6
essay/'eseɪ/ 3.6
evidence/'evɪdəns/ 3.8
exaggerate/ɪg'zædʒəreɪt/ 2.10
exam/ɪg'zæm/ 3.6
exchange/ɪks'tʃeɪndʒ/ 3.4
exciting/ɪk'saɪtɪŋ/ 2.3
exhausted/ɪg'zɔːstɪd/ 1.3
exhibition/ˌeksɪ'bɪʃən/ 2.4
expensive/ɪk'spensɪv/ 3.4
fail (a test/an exam)/'feɪl (ə
ˌtest, ən ɪgˌzæm)/ 3.6
faint/feɪnt/ 3.7
fall asleep/ˌfɔːl ə'sliːp/ 1.3
fare/feər/ 3.5
fashionable/'fæʃənəbəl/ 1.10
feed/fiːd/ 3.2
fees/fiːz/ 3.5
fence/fens/ 1.1
fertilize/'fɜːtɪlaɪz/ 3.2
fiction/'fɪkʃən/ 2.9
field/fiːld/ 3.2
film/fɪlm/ 2.8

film director/'fɪlm dɪˌrektər/ 2.6
film star/'fɪlm stɑːr/ 2.6
filthy/'fɪlθi/ 1.5
fireplace/'faɪəpleɪs/ 1.1
floor/flɔːr/ 1.1
floral/'flɔːrəl/ 1.10
florist's/'flɒrɪsts/ 3.4
flute/fluːt/ 2.7
folk/fəʊk/ 2.7
football/'fʊtbɔːl/ 2.1
forgive/fə'gɪv/ 2.10
fork/fɔːk/ 1.7
foul/faʊl/ 2.2
fresh/freʃ/ 1.8
front door/ˌfrʌnt 'dɔːr/ 1.1
front garden/ˌfrʌnt 'gɑːdn/ 1.1
frozen/'frəʊzən/ 1.8
fry/fraɪ/ 1.6
frying pan/'fraɪ-ɪŋ ˌpæn/ 1.6
fun/fʌn/ 2.3, 2.5
funny/'fʌni/ 2.5
galaxy/'gæləksi/ 3.10
gambler/'gæmblər/ 2.4
garage/'gærɑːʒ/ 1.1
garden/'gɑːdn/ 1.1
gate/geɪt/ 1.1
gatecrash/'geɪtkræʃ/ 2.3
gather/'gæðər/ 3.2
get up/ˌget 'ʌp/ 1.3
give a lecture/ˌgɪv ə 'lektʃər/ 2.10
give a party/ˌgɪv ə 'pɑːti/ 2.3
give a present/ˌgɪv ə
'prezənt/ 2.3
give a speech/ˌgɪv ə 'spiːtʃ/ 2.10
give evidence/ˌgɪv 'evɪdəns/ 3.8
glass/glɑːs/ 1.7, 1.8
glossary/'glɒsəri/ 2.9
glove/glʌv/ 1.9
glue/gluː/ 3.3
go bad/gəʊ 'bæd/ 1.8
golf/gɒlf/ 2.1
go off/gəʊ 'ɒf/ 1.8
go on trial/gəʊ ɒn 'traɪəl/ 3.8
go rotten/gəʊ 'rɒtn/ 1.8
go sour/gəʊ 'saʊər/ 1.8
gossip/'gɒsɪp/ 2.10
go stale/gəʊ 'steɪl/ 1.8
go to bed/gəʊ tə 'bed/ 1.3
govern/'gʌvən/ 3.9
government/'gʌvəmənt/ 3.9
go wild/gəʊ 'waɪld/ 2.3
grape/greɪp/ 1.6
grate/greɪt/ 1.6
greengrocer's
/'griːnˌgrəʊsəz/ 3.4
group/gruːp/ 2.7
guarantee/ˌgærən'tiː/ 3.4
guilty/'gɪlti/ 3.8
guitar/gɪ'tɑːr/ 2.7
gymnastics/dʒɪm'næstɪks/ 2.1
hall/hɔːl/ 1.1
ham/hæm/ 1.6
hammer/'hæmər/ 3.3

handball/'hændbɔːl/ 2.1
hardware store/'hɑːdweər
stɔːr/ 3.4
harvest/'hɑːvɪst/ 3.2
hat/hæt/ 1.9
have a good time/ˌhæv ə
gʊd 'taɪm/ 2.3
have fun/ˌhæv 'fʌn/ 2.3
headache/'hedeɪk/ 3.7
headline/'hedlaɪn/ 2.9
heat/hiːt/ 1.6
hedge/hedʒ/ 1.1
hen/hen/ 3.2
high-heeled/'haɪ-hiːld/ 1.10
hijacking/'haɪdʒækɪŋ/ 3.8
hit/hɪt/ 2.2
hockey/'hɒki/ 2.1
horse riding/'hɔːs ˌraɪdɪŋ/ 2.1
humorous/'hjuːmərəs/ 2.5
hurt/hɜːt/ 3.7
in adj/ɪn/ 1.10
in a mess/ˌɪn ə 'mes/ 1.5
in fashion/ɪn 'fæʃən/ 1.10
index/'ɪndeks/ 2.9
industrial/ɪn'dʌstriəl/ 3.9
industry/'ɪndəstri/ 3.9
insomnia/ɪn'sɒmniə/ 3.7
interest/'ɪntrəst/ 3.5
introduction/ˌɪntrə'dʌkʃən/ 2.9
invest/ɪn'vest/ 3.5
invite/ɪn'vaɪt/ 2.3
iron/'aɪən/ 1.5
jacket/'dʒækɪt/ 1.9
jar/dʒɑːr/ 1.8
jazz/dʒæz/ 2.7
jeans/dʒiːnz/ 1.9
jeweller's/'dʒuːələz/ 3.4
job/dʒɒb/ 3.1
joke/dʒəʊk/ 2.5
judge/dʒʌdʒ/ 3.8
judo/'dʒuːdəʊ/ 2.1
jump/dʒʌmp/ 2.2
jury/'dʒʊəri/ 3.8
kettle/'ketl/ 1.8
kick/kɪk/ 2.2
kid/kɪd/ 2.5
kidnapping/'kɪdnæpɪŋ/ 3.8
kindergarten/'kɪndəgɑːtn/ 3.6
king/kɪŋ/ 3.9
kitchen/'kɪtʃən/ 1.1
knife/naɪf/ 1.6, 1.7,
3.3
ladder/'lædər/ 3.3
lamb/læm/ 1.6
lamp/læmp/ 1.2
launch/lɔːntʃ/ 3.10
lecture/'lektʃər/ 2.10
lend/lend/ 3.5
lesson/'lesən/ 3.6
lick/lɪk/ 1.7
linoleum/lɪ'nəʊliəm/ 1.2
lipstick/'lɪpstɪk/ 1.4
living room/'lɪvɪŋ ruːm/ 1.1

Term	Ref.
loss /lɒs/	3.5
low price /ˈləʊ praɪs/	3.4
magazine /ˌmægəˈziːn/	2.9
magician /məˈdʒɪʃən/	2.6
make a loss /ˌmeɪk ə ˈlɒs/	3.5
make a profit /ˌmeɪk ə ˈprɒfɪt/	3.5
make a pun /ˌmeɪk ə ˈpʌn/	2.5
make fun of /ˌmeɪk ˈfʌn əv/	2.5
make money /ˌmeɪk ˈmʌni/	3.5
make the bed /ˌmeɪk ðə ˈbed/	1.5
make-up /ˈmeɪk-ʌp/	1.4
manager /ˈmænɪdʒər/	3.1
manure /məˈnjʊər/	3.2
mat /mæt/	1.2
match /mætʃ/	2.2
mattress /ˈmætrɪs/	1.3
melody /ˈmelədi/	2.7
melt /melt/	1.6
mess /mes/	1.5
mix /mɪks/	1.6
money /ˈmʌni/	3.5
moon /muːn/	3.10
mop /mɒp/	1.5
movie /ˈmuːvi/	2.8
mug /mʌg/	1.7, 1.8
mumble /ˈmʌmbəl/	2.10
museum /mjuːˈzɪəm/	2.4
musician /mjuːˈzɪʃən/	2.6
nail /neɪl/	3.3
nail polish /ˈneɪl ˌpɒlɪʃ/	1.4
napkin /ˈnæpkɪn/	1.7
neat /niːt/	1.5
news /njuːz/	2.8
newsagent's /ˈnjuːzˌeɪdʒənts/	3.4
newspaper /ˈnjuːsˌpeɪpər/	2.9
nightmare /ˈnaɪtmeər/	1.3
non-fiction /nɒn ˈfɪkʃən/	2.9
notes /nəʊts/	3.6
novel /ˈnɒvəl/	2.9
nurse /nɜːs/	3.1
nut /nʌt/	3.3
off /ɒf/	1.8, 3.4
office worker /ˈɒfɪs wɜːkər/	3.1
off-licence /ˈɒf laɪsəns/	3.4
old-fashioned /ˌəʊld ˈfæʃənd/	1.10
opera /ˈɒpərə/	2.4
orbit /ˈɔːbɪt/	3.10
orchestra /ˈɔːkɪstrə/	2.4
organ /ˈɔːgən/	2.7
out-dated /ˌaʊt ˈdeɪtɪd/	1.10
out of breath /ˌaʊt əv ˈbreθ/	3.7
out of fashion /ˌaʊt əv ˈfæʃən/	1.10
out of work /ˌaʊt əv ˈwɜːk/	3.1
oven /ˈʌvən/	1.6
overcoat /ˈəʊvəkəʊt/	1.9
owe /əʊ/	3.5
own /əʊn/	3.5
packet /ˈpækɪt/	1.8
pain /peɪn/	3.7
paperback /ˈpeɪpəbæk/	2.9
parliament /ˈpɑːləmənt/	3.9
party /ˈpɑːti/	2.3, 3.9
pass /pɑːs/	2.2
pass (a test/an exam) /pɑːs ə ˈtest, ən ɪgˈzæm/	3.6
pass sentence /ˌpɑːs ˈsentəns/	3.8
path /pɑːθ/	1.1
pay back /peɪ bæk/	3.5
pea /piː/	1.6
peach /piːtʃ/	1.6
pear /peər/	1.6
peel /piːl/	1.6
pension /ˈpenʃən/	3.5
perfume /ˈpɜːfjuːm/	1.4
piano /piˈænəʊ/	2.7
pick /pɪk/	3.2
pillow /ˈpɪləʊ/	1.3
pineapple /ˈpaɪnæpl/	1.6
planet /ˈplænɪt/	3.10
plant /plɑːnt/	3.2
plate /pleɪt/	1.7
play /pleɪ/	2.9
play a joke on /pleɪ ə ˈdʒəʊk ɒn/	2.5
pleated /ˈpliːtɪd/	1.10
pliers /ˈplaɪəz/	3.3
plough /plaʊ/	3.2
plum /plʌm/	1.6
poem /ˈpəʊɪm/	2.9
polish /ˈpɒlɪʃ/	1.5
political /pəˈlɪtɪkəl/	3.9
political party /pəˌlɪtɪkəl ˈpɑːti/	3.9
politician /ˌpɒlɪˈtɪʃən/	3.9
politics /ˈpɒlɪtɪks/	3.9
polo neck /ˈpəʊləʊ nek/	1.10
pop /pɒp/	2.7
pop star /ˈpɒp stɑːr/	2.6
pour /pɔːr/	1.6
president /ˈprezɪdənt/	3.9
price /praɪs/	3.4
prime minister /ˌpraɪm ˈmɪnɪstər/	3.9
prince /prɪns/	3.9
princess /ˌprɪnˈses/	3.9
prison /ˈprɪzən/	3.8
profession /prəˈfeʃən/	3.1
profit /ˈprɒfɪt/	3.5
programme /ˈprəʊgræm/	2.8
promise /ˈprɒmɪs/	2.10
prosecution /ˌprɒsɪˈkjuːʃən/	3.8
pull someone's leg /ˌpʊl ˈsʌmwʌnz ˈleg/	2.5
pun /pʌn/	2.5
punk /pʌŋk/	2.7
pupil /ˈpjuːpəl/	3.6
purchase /ˈpɜːtʃɪs/	3.5
pyjamas /pəˈdʒɑːməz/	1.3
queen /kwiːn/	3.9
quiz show /ˈkwɪz ʃəʊ/	2.8
radio /ˈreɪdiəʊ/	1.2
rape /reɪp/	3.8
raw /rɔː/	1.8
reach a verdict /ˌriːtʃ ə ˈvɜːdɪkt/	3.8
reap /riːp/	3.2
receipt /rɪˈsiːt/	3.4
record /ˈrekɔːd/	1.2
reduced /rɪˈdjuːst/	3.4
reduction /rɪˈdʌkʃən/	3.4
referee /ˌrefəˈriː/	2.2
refund /ˈriːfʌnd/	3.4
reggae /ˈregeɪ/	2.7
release from prison /rɪˈliːs frəm ˈprɪzən/	3.8
rent /rent/	3.5
repay /rɪˈpeɪ/	3.5
republic /rɪˈpʌblɪk/	3.9
retail price /ˈriːteɪl praɪs/	3.4
rhythm /ˈrɪðəm/	2.7
riddle /ˈrɪdl/	2.5
rock /rɒk/	2.7
rocket /ˈrɒkɪt/	3.10
roof /ruːf/	1.1
rotten /ˈrɒtn/	1.8
rowing /ˈrəʊɪŋ/	2.1
royal family /ˌrɔɪəl ˈfæməli/	3.9
rug /rʌg/	1.2
rugby /ˈrʌgbi/	2.1
run /rʌn/	2.2
sailing /ˈseɪlɪŋ/	2.1
salary /ˈsæləri/	3.5
sale /seɪl/	3.4
sales representative /ˈseɪlz reprɪˌzentətɪv/	3.1
salesperson /ˈseɪlzpɜːsən/	3.1
salted /ˈsɔːltɪd/	1.8
satellite /ˈsætəlaɪt/	3.10
saucepan /ˈsɔːspæn/	1.6
saucer /ˈsɔːsər/	1.7
sausage /ˈsɒsɪdʒ/	1.6
save /seɪv/	3.5
saw /sɔː/	3.3
saxophone /ˈsæksəfəʊn/	2.7
scarf /skɑːf/	1.9
schoolchild, schoolchildren /ˈskuːltʃaɪld, ˈskuːltʃɪldrən/	3.6
score /skɔːr/	2.2
screen /skriːn/	2.4
screw /skruː/	3.3
screwdriver /ˈskruːˌdraɪvər/	3.3
scrub /skrʌb/	1.5
scrubbing brush /ˈskrʌbɪŋ brʌʃ/	1.5
secondary school /ˈsekəndəri skuːl/	3.6
secretary /ˈsekrɪtəri/	3.1
see the sights /siː ðə ˈsaɪts/	2.4
send into orbit /ˌsend ɪntʊ ˈɔːbɪt/	3.10
send to prison /ˌsend tə ˈprɪzən/	3.8
sentence /ˈsentəns/	3.8
series /ˈsɪəriːz/	2.7
serve /sɜːv/	2.2

set /set/ 2.2
shampoo /ʃæm'puː/ 1.4
shaving cream /'ʃeɪvɪŋ kriːm/ 1.4
sheet /ʃiːt/ 1.3
shelf /ʃelf/ 1.2
shepherd /'ʃepəd/ 3.2
shine /ʃaɪn/ 1.5
shirt /ʃɜːt/ 1.9
shoe /ʃuː/ 1.9
shoot /ʃuːt/ 2.2
shooting /'ʃuːtɪŋ/ 2.1
shoplifting /'ʃɒpˌlɪftɪŋ/ 3.8
shorts /ʃɔːts/ 1.9
short-sleeved /ˌʃɔːt 'sliːvd/ 1.10
shout /ʃaʊt/ 2.10
show /ʃəʊ/ 2.8
sights /saɪts/ 2.4
sightseeing /'saɪtˌsiːɪŋ/ 2.4
silly /'sɪli/ 2.5
singer /'sɪŋər/ 2.6
skilled /skɪld/ 3.1
skirt /skɜːt/ 1.9
sleepy /'sliːpi/ 1.3
slice /slaɪs/ 1.6
smoked /sməʊkt/ 1.8
smuggling /'smʌɡlɪŋ/ 3.8
soap opera /'səʊp ˌɒpərə/ 2.8
social /'səʊʃəl/ 3.9
society /sə'saɪəti/ 3.9
sock /sɒk/ 1.9
sofa /'səʊfə/ 1.2
soil /sɔɪl/ 3.2
solar system /'səʊlər ˌsɪstəm/ 3.10
sore throat /sɔː 'θrəʊt/ 3.7
sour /saʊr/ 1.8
spacecraft /'speɪsˌkrɑːft/ 3.10
spaceship /'speɪsˌʃɪp/ 3.10
space shuttle /'speɪs ˌʃʌtl/ 3.10
space station /'speɪs ˌsteɪʃən/ 3.10
space travel /'speɪs ˌtrævəl/ 3.10
spade /speɪd/ 3.3
spanner /'spænər/ 3.3
speech /spiːtʃ/ 2.10
spend /spend/ 3.5
spinach /'spɪnɪdʒ/ 1.6
spoon /spuːn/ 1.6, 1.7
sports show /'spɔːts ʃəʊ/ 2.8
spotless /'spɒtləs/ 1.5
spray /spreɪ/ 3.2
stadium /'steɪdiəm/ 2.2
stage /steɪdʒ/ 2.4
stale /steɪl/ 1.8
star /stɑːr/ 2.6, 3.10
stationer's /'steɪʃənəz/ 3.4
stay at home /ˌsteɪ ət 'həʊm/ 2.4
steak /steɪk/ 1.6
stereo system /'steriəʊ ˌsɪstəm/ 1.2
stick v /stɪk/ 3.3
stir /stɜːr/ 1.6
stool /stuːl/ 1.2
store /stɔːr/ 3.2
storey /'stɔːri/ 1.1

story /'stɔːri/ 2.9
stove /stəʊv/ 1.6
straw /strɔː/ 1.7
strawberry /'strɔːbəri/ 1.6
string /strɪŋ/ 3.3
striped /straɪpt/ 1.10
student /'stjuːdənt/ 3.6
study /'stʌdi/ 3.6
stunt man/woman /'stʌnt mæn, -wʊmən/ 2.6
stutter /'stʌtər/ 2.10
stylish /'staɪlɪʃ/ 1.10
suck /sʌk/ 1.7
suit /suːt/ 1.9
supermarket /'suːpəˌmɑːkət/ 3.4
sweater /'swetər/ 1.9
sweep /swiːp/ 1.5
swimming /'swɪmɪŋ/ 2.1
switch /swɪtʃ/ 1.2
table /'teɪbl/ 1.2
tablecloth /'teɪbəlklɒθ/ 1.7
table tennis /'teɪbl ˌtenəs/ 2.1
tackle /'tækl/ 2.2
take a bite /ˌteɪk ə 'baɪt/ 1.7
take (a test/an exam) /ˌteɪk (ə 'test, ən ɪɡˌzæm)/ 3.6
take notes /teɪk 'nəʊts/ 3.6
talk show /'tɔːk ʃəʊ/ 2.8
tap /tæp/ 1.4
tax /tæks/ 3.5
teacher /'tiːtʃər/ 3.1
tease /tiːz/ 2.5
television personality /'telɪˌvɪʒən pɜːsəˈnæləti/ 2.6
television set /'telɪˌvɪʒən set/ 1.2
tell a joke /ˌtel ə 'dʒəʊk/ 2.5
tell a riddle /ˌtel ə 'rɪdl/ 2.5
temperature /'tempərətʃər/ 3.7
tennis /'tenəs/ 2.1
tennis shoes /'tenəs ʃuːz/ 1.9
test /test/ 3.6
textbook /'tekstbʊk/ 2.9
theatre /'θɪətər/ 2.4
threaten /'θretn/ 2.10
throat /θrəʊt/ 3.7
throw /θrəʊ/ 2.2
tidy /'taɪdi/ 1.5
tie n /taɪ/ 1.9
tie v /taɪ/ 3.3
tight-fitting /ˌtaɪt'fɪtɪŋ/ 1.10
tighten /'taɪtn/ 3.3
tin /tɪn/ 1.8
tinned /tɪnd/ 1.8
tired /taɪəd/ 1.3
title /'taɪtl/ 2.9
toothbrush /'tuːθbrʌʃ/ 1.4
toothpaste /'tuːθpeɪst/ 1.4
towel /'taʊəl/ 1.4
tractor /'træktər/ 3.2
traditional /trə'dɪʃənəl/ 1.10
trendy /'trendi/ 1.10
trial /'traɪəl/ 3.8
trip /trɪp/ 2.4

trousers /'traʊzəz/ 1.9
trumpet /'trʌmpət/ 2.7
T-shirt /'tiːʃɜːt/ 1.9
tune /tjuːn/ 2.7
turkey /'tɜːki/ 1.6
umpire /'ʌmpaɪər/ 2.2
unconsciousness /ʌn'kɒnʃəs/ 1.3
undergraduate /ˌʌndə'ɡrædʒuət/ 3.6
underpants /'ʌndəpænts/ 1.9
underwear /'ʌndəweər/ 1.9
unemployed /ˌʌnɪm'plɔɪd/ 3.1
unfashionable /ˌʌn'fæʃənəbəl/ 1.10
universe /'juːnɪvɜːs/ 3.10
university /ˌjuːnɪ'vɜːsəti/ 3.6
unskilled /ˌʌn'skɪld/ 3.1
untidy /ˌʌn'taɪdi/ 1.5
upstairs /ˌʌp'steəz/ 1.1
vacuum cleaner /'vækjʊəm ˌkliːnər/ 1.5
veal /viːl/ 1.6
verdict /'vɜːdɪkt/ 3.8
vineyard /'vɪnjəd/ 3.2
violin /ˌvaɪə'lɪn/ 2.7
V-neck /'viː nek/ 1.10
volleyball /'vɒlibɔːl/ 2.1
vomit /'vɒmət/ 3.7
vote /vəʊt/ 3.9
voter /'vəʊtər/ 3.9
wages /'weɪdʒəz/ 3.5
waiter /'weɪtər/ 2.4
wake up /ˌweɪk 'ʌp/ 1.3
walk /wɔːk/ 2.4
wall /wɔːl/ 1.1
wardrobe /'wɔːdrəʊb/ 1.2
warn /wɔːn/ 2.10
wash /wɒʃ/ 1.4
washbasin /'wɒʃ ˌbeɪsən/ 1.4
washing machine /'wɒʃɪŋ məˌʃiːn/ 1.5
washing-up /ˌwɒʃɪŋ 'ʌp/ 1.5
water v /'wɔːtər/ 3.2
weightlifting /'weɪtˌlɪftɪŋ/ 2.1
wheat /wiːt/ 3.2
whisper /'wɪspər/ 2.10
white-collar /ˌwaɪt 'kɒlər/ 3.1
wholesale price /'həʊlseɪl praɪs/ 3.4
window /'wɪndəʊ/ 1.1
window-shopping /'wɪndəʊˌʃɒpɪŋ/ 2.4
windsurfing /'wɪndˌsɜːfɪŋ/ 2.1
wipe /waɪp/ 1.5
wire /waɪər/ 3.3
witness /'wɪtnəs/ 3.8
witty /'wɪti/ 2.5
worth /wɜːθ/ 3.5
wound /wuːnd/ 3.7
wrestling /'reslɪŋ/ 2.1
zoo /zuː/ 2.4

Key

Unit 1.1

Exercise 1

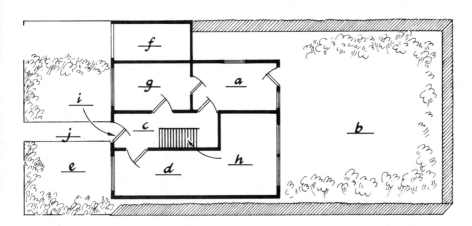

Exercise 2

1) e   2) h   3) b   4) g   5) f   6) a   7) d   8) c

Exercise 3

1) stairs – the other three are the sides of a room
2) roof – the other three are parts of a heating system
3) garage – the other three are rooms inside a house
4) wall – the other three are openings
5) storey – the other three are specific areas in a house
6) path – the other three are vertical structures

Just for fun

There are various possible answers to this exercise.

Unit 1.2

Exercise 1

The following do not exist in the 25th century:

1) **books** (the child says 'what are those things . . . are they books?' – the child had heard of books but had never seen any before.)   2) **coffee** (the guide says it was made illegal 200 years ago)   3) **televisions** (the child says 'What's that box?')   7) **records** (the guide has to explain what they are)   10) **sofas** (the guide explains what they are)   13) **cigarettes** (same as for coffee above)   15) **Mickey Mouse films**

Exercise 2

1) g   2) d   3) h   4) a   5) f   6) b   7) c   8) e

Exercise 3

1) shelf   2) stereo system   3) coffee table   4) ashtray   5) cassette recorder
6) window

Dictionary work

to sit on	**to put things in**	**to walk on**
a deckchair	a cupboard	a rug
a bench	a chest of drawers	a mat
a stool	a wardrobe	a carpet
a cushion	a cabinet	lino

Unit 1.3

Exercise 1

1 1) pillow   2) sheet   3) mattress   4) pyjamas   5) blanket
2 Diagram 4 shows a normal night's sleep.

Exercise 2

1) d   2) f   3) b   4) c   5) g   6) a   7) e

Exercise 3

1) e   2) f   3) d   4) b   5) a   6) c

Just for fun

There are various possible answers to this exercise.

Unit 1.4

Exercise 1

1 Nowadays most homes have bathrooms.
2 In the past most people never brushed their teeth.
3 Nowadays most people wash every day.
4 In the past most people didn't use soap.
5 In the past most kings and queens of Europe didn't have baths.
6 Nowadays most people believe that it is important to be clean.
7 In the past most people needed to wear perfume.

Exercise 2

1) toothbrush used for brushing your teeth   2) soap used for washing yourself   3) towel used for drying yourself   4) bath used for having a bath

Exercise 3

1) c   2) a   3) d   4) e   5) f   6) b

Dictionary work

1) g   2) a   3) d   4) c   5) b   6) e   7) f

Unit 1.5

Exercise 1

1) e   2) b   3) d   4) g   5) c   6) a   7) f

Exercise 2

1 untidy is similar in meaning to in a mess
2 tidy is similar in meaning to neat
3 spotless means very very clean
4 filthy means very very dirty

Exercise 3

1) d   2) a   3) h   4) i   5) b   6) g   7) c   8) f   9) e

Just for fun

There are various possible answers to this exercise.

Test yourself 1

1) armchair   2) garage   3) ceiling   4) spotless   5) toothpaste   6) polish
7) cushion   8) blanket   9) perfume   10) filthy   11) hall   12) mattress
13) mess   14) towel   15) path   16) nightmare   17) curtains   18) dishwasher
19) soap   20) roof   21) exhausted   22) drowsy/sleepy   23) switch   24) make-up
25) desk

Unit 1.6

Exercise 1

1) fried   2) scrambled   3) boiled   4) baked   5) egg salad

Exercise 2

1) oven   2) knife   3) frying pan   4) stove   5) spoon   6) saucepan   7) knife
8) spoon   9) knife

Exercise 3

1) d, f   2) a   3) a, g   4) e   5) d, f   6) a, c, g   7) a, b, e   8) a, b, c, g

Dictionary work

M	sausage	M	ham	F	grape	V	pea	V	bean
F	pineapple	V	celery	M	lamb	V	cabbage	M	chop
F	strawberry	M	steak	F	peach	V	spinach	F	avocado
M	turkey	M	veal	F	pear	V	cucumber	F	plum

Unit 1.7

Exercise 1

a) 4   b) 3   c) 9   d) 7   e) 1

Exercise 2

1) e   2) k   3) a   4) h   5) j   6) b   7) l   8) i   9) d   10) c   11) g   12) f

Just for fun

There are various possible answers to this exercise.

Unit 1.8

Exercise 1

1) bad   2) thousands   3) nineteenth   4) fresh   5) jars   6) metal   7) refrigerator   8) sour   9) off
10) frozen

Exercise 2

sour	**rotten**	**stale**	**off**
1 cream	3 tomatoes	5 cake	7 ham
2 milk	4 bananas	6 biscuits	8 chicken

Exercise 3

1) f   2) e   3) a   4) c   5) h   6) b   7) d   8) g

Dictionary work

1) i   2) c   3) d   4) j   5) h   6) g   7) a   8) f   9) l   10) e   11) b   12) k

Unit 1.9

Exercise 1

1) T   2) F   3) T   4) F   5) F   6) T

Exercise 2

1) glove   2) trousers   3) hat   4) boot   5) jacket   6) sock

Exercise 3

Chart 1

	above waist	below waist	above and below
1 underpants		X	
2 suit			X
3 dress			X
4 tie	X		
5 shorts		X	
6 scarf	X		
7 skirt		X	
8 underwear			X
9 shirt	X		

Chart 2

	women only	both men and women
1 T-shirt		X
2 underwear		X
3 jeans		X
4 blouse	X	
5 dress	X	
6 boots		X
7 jacket		X
8 gloves		X
9 skirt	X	

Just for fun

There are various possible answers to this exercise. Here is one possible set of answers.
1) shirt – the other three come in pairs
2) socks – the other three go over the legs not on the feet
3) underpants – the other three can usually be seen when you wear them
4) tie – the other three are usually worn when you are outdoors
5) T-shirt – the other three are usually worn on more formal occasions

Unit 1.10

Exercise 1
1) b   2) b   3) a   4) a   5) b

Exercise 2

modern	**old**
in fashion	old-fashioned
stylish	conservative
trendy	out-dated
in	out of fashion

Exercise 3
1) trendy   2) traditional   3) unfashionable   4) stylish

Dictionary work
1) j   2) l   3) d   4) k   5) b   6) a   7) h   8) e   9) i   10) c   11) g   12) f

Test yourself 2
1) stylish   2) boils   3) chew   4) tie   5) old-fashioned   6) raw   7) stir   8) lick   9) fashion   10) stale
11) suit   12) ham   13) trendy   14) box   15) napkins   16) hat   17) frozen   18) melt   19) sucking
20) jar   21) dress   22) striped   23) oven   24) plate   25) boots

Unit 2.1

Exercise 1
1) 1896, Athens   2) 1936, Berlin   3) 1904, St. Louis   4) 1988, Seoul   5) 1964, Tokyo   6) 1896, Athens
7) 1908, London   8) 1964, Tokyo   9) 1984, Los Angeles

Exercise 2

sports played in teams	sports that can be played against one other person	sports that can be played alone
volleyball	judo	sailing
handball	boxing	golf
football	table tennis	swimming
basketball	tennis	cycling

Exercise 3
1) weightlifting   2) horse riding   3) shooting   4) gymnastics   5) rowing   6) rugby

Just for fun
There are various possible answers to this exercise. Here is one possible set of answers.
1) tennis – all the others are team sports
2) volleyball – the other three involve fighting
3) table tennis – the other three you can do alone
4) basketball – in the other three you have to get a ball over a net
5) football – to do the other three you need some sort of bat or club
6) swimming – to do the other three you need some sort of boat or watercraft

Unit 2.2

Exercise 1
1) OK   2) Not OK   3) OK   4) Not OK

Exercise 2
1) f   2) h   3) d   4) b   5) e   6) a   7) g   8) c

Exercise 3
1) b, e, f, g   2) a, c, d   3) b   4) e, g   5) a, c, f   6) b, e   7) d   8) b, g

Dictionary work
1) g   2) d   3) b   4) f   5) a   6) c   7) h   8) e

Unit 2.3

Exercise 1
1) party   2) dance   3) enjoying   4) invited   5) friend   6) celebrate   7) fun   8) different   9) boring
10) crazy   11) cake   12) mother

Exercise 2
1) D   2) S   3) S   4) D   5) S   6) D   7) S   8) D   9) S   10) D

Just for fun
There are various possible answers to this exercise.

Unit 2.4

Exercise 1
1) i   2) f   3) d   4) a   5) j   6) g   7) b   8) h   9) c   10) e

Exercise 2
1) to a   2) 0   3) a   4) 0   5) for a   6) on a   7) to the   8) for   9) the   10) at

Exercise 3
1) e   2) g   3) a   4) c   5) f   6) d   7) b

Dictionary work
1) i   2) f   3) j   4) c   5) b   6) a   7) g   8) d   9) h   10) e

Unit 2.5

Exercise 1
1) riddles   2) amusing   3) joke   4) witty   5) true   6) kidding   7) friendly   8) silly

Exercise 2
1) A   2) A   3) B   4) B   5) A   6) B

Exercise 3
1) c   2) d   3) b   4) a   5) e

Just for fun
You tell a joke!

Test yourself 3
1) tease   2) sightseeing   3) cycling   4) scored   5) stage   6) invite   7) kidding   8) weightlifting
9) competition   10) joke   11) basketball   12) trip   13) presents   14) witty/funny   15) net   16) enjoy
17) sailing   18) celebrate   19) amusing   20) referee   21) museum   22) shoot   23) boring
24) gymnastics   25) casino

Unit 2.6

Exercise 1
1) T   2) T   3) T   4) F   5) F   6) F   7) T   8) F

Exercise 2
1) clown   2) film director   3) actress   4) magician   5) stunt man

Exercise 3
1) d   2) c   3) g   4) f   5) b   6) a   7) e

Just for fun
There are various possible answers to this exercise.

Unit 2.7

Exercise 1
1) c   2) e   3) f   4) g   5) a   6) d   7) b

Exercise 2
1) group *or* 2) band   3) melody *or* 4) tune   5) rhythm *or* 6) beat

Exercise 3

	pop	punk	folk	reggae	jazz	classical
1 often played by a big orchestra in a concert hall						X
2 often played by young people with guitars in a group	X	X	X	X		
3 often played by young people with brightly coloured hair		X				
4 often simple tunes which are popular for a short time	X	X				
5 music coming originally from black American musicians					X	
6 music of a specific region, popular for a very long time			X			
7 music with a strong regular rhythm, originally from Jamaica				X		
8 music which is popular for dancing in discos	X	X		X		
9 often played freely, not following written music					X	

Dictionary work
1) e   2) d   3) f   4) b   5) c   6) a   7) h   8) g

Unit 2.8

Exercise 1
1) a   2) d   3) c   4) c   5) a   6) b   7) a   8) c

Exercise 2
1) i   2) d   3) f   4) g   5) a   6) e   7) c   8) j   9) b   10) h

Just for fun
Design your own evening of television.

Unit 2.9

Exercise 1
1) b   2) b   3) a   4) a   5) c

Exercise 2
fiction: novel, short story, play, poem
non-fiction: atlas, textbook, dictionary, encyclopedia

Exercise 3
1) f   2) c   3) e   4) i   5) a   6) g   7) h   8) d   9) b

Dictionary work
1) T   2) N   3) T   4) N   5) T   6) N   7) N   8) N   9) T   10) T   11) N   12) T

Unit 2.10

Exercise 1
1) b   2) c   3) b   4) c

Exercise 2
1) e   2) g   3) b   4) f   5) j   6) a   7) h   8) i   9) c   10) d

Dictionary work
1) i   2) f   3) d   4) b   5) l   6) g   7) e   8) k   9) h   10) a   11) j   12) c

Test yourself 4

1) classical 2) comedians 3) news 4) advise 5) chapter 6) channels 7) pop 8) index
9) actress 10) speech 11) drums 12) magicians 13) headline 14) series 15) mumble
16) film director 17) poems 18) documentary 19) beat 20) whisper 21) clowns 22) group 23) chat
24) magazine 25) advertisements

Unit 3.1

Exercise 1

	Martha	George	Billy	No one
1 Who had a white-collar job for a while?		X		
2 Who works in a profession?	X			
3 Who wanted to become a secretary?				X
4 Who is unemployed at the moment?				X
5 Who is an unskilled worker?			X	
6 Who was a successful salesperson?		X		
7 Who wanted a different career as a child?	X			
8 Who married the boss?				X
9 Who has no career?			X	
10 Who was out of work for a while?			X	

Exercise 2

1) blue-collar worker is similar in meaning to factory worker
2) unemployed is similar in meaning to out of work
3) boss is similar in meaning to manager
4) office worker is similar in meaning to white-collar worker

Exercise 3

	professional worker	white-collar worker	skilled worker
1 engineer	X		
2 secretary		X	
3 bank cashier		X	
4 architect	X		
5 teacher	X		
6 mechanic			X
7 lawyer	X		
8 computer repair person			X
9 office manager		X	
10 hairdresser			X

Just for fun

There are various possible answers to this exercise.

Unit 3.2

Exercise 1

	spring	summer	autumn	winter
1 The fields are planted.	X			
2 The fruit is picked.			X	
3 The crops are sprayed.		X		
4 The corn is reaped.			X	
5 The fields are planned.				X
6 The wood is chopped.				X
7 The crops are stored in the barns.				X
8 The fields are ploughed.	X			
9 The fields are watered.		X		
10 The fields are fertilized.	X			

Exercise 2

1) b   2) f   3) e   4) g   5) a   6) d   7) c

Exercise 3

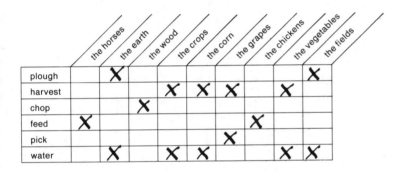

	the horses	the earth	the wood	the crops	the corn	the grapes	the chickens	the vegetables	the fields
plough		X							X
harvest				X	X	X		X	
chop			X						
feed	X						X		
pick						X			
water		X		X	X			X	X

Dictionary work

1) j   2) h   3) e   4) a   5) k   6) c   7) b   8) l   9) f   10) i   11) g   12) d

Unit 3.3

Exercise 1

a) 4   b) 3   c) 5   d) 6   e) 2   f) 1

Exercise 2

tools: hammer, spanner, saw, screwdriver
things used with tools: screw, nail, glue, bolt

Exercise 3

1) d   2) a   3) f   4) e   5) b   6) c

Just for fun

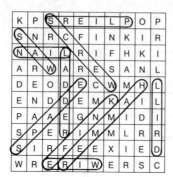

K	P	S	R	E	I	L	P	O	P
S	N	R	C	F	I	N	K	I	R
N	A	I	L	R	I	F	H	K	I
A	R	W	A	R	E	S	A	N	L
D	E	O	D	E	C	W	M	H	L
E	N	D	D	E	M	K	A	I	L
P	A	A	E	G	N	M	I	D	I
S	P	E	R	I	M	M	L	R	R
S	I	R	F	E	E	X	I	E	D
W	R	E	R	I	W	E	R	S	C

Unit 3.4

Exercise 1
1) F   2) T   3) T   4) T   5) F   6) F   7) T   8) F   9) F   10) T

Exercise 2
1) S   2) S   3) D   4) D   5) S   6) D

Exercise 3
1) e   2) a   3) d   4) g   5) b   6) c   7) f

Dictionary work
1) g   2) j   3) e   4) c   5) k   6) i   7) a   8) h   9) l   10) f   11) b   12) d

Unit 3.5

Exercise 1
1) e   2) g   3) h   4) c   5) a   6) d   7) b   8) f

Exercise 2
1) a   2) b   3) a   4) b   5) a

Exercise 3

In Britain and the United States, many people would like to __own__ their own homes, but it is usually very difficult to __save__ enough money. Most people __spend__ as much as they __earn__ each month. But if you can't __afford__ to buy a house, often you can get a bank to __lend__ you the money to buy one. The bank knows that a house is a very good place for you to __invest__ your money. A few years after you buy it, a house is usually __worth__ much more than it originally __cost__ you, so you can __sell__ it for a big profit.

Dictionary work
1) f   2) c   3) a   4) i   5) d   6) b   7) e   8) g   9) j   10) h

Test yourself 5

1) afford   2) harvest   3) profession   4) unskilled   5) department   6) boss   7) cheque   8) cattle
9) discount   10) screwdriver   11) salesperson   12) saw   13) planted   14) bargain   15) taxes   16) nails
17) tractor   18) lend   19) glue   20) unemployed   21) ladder   22) pick   23) receipt   24) owe
25) interest

Unit 3.6

Exercise 1
1) b   2) c   3) a   4) a   5) a   6) c

Exercise 2

place for learning	person who studies	something produced by a student
college	*undergraduate*	*essay*
kindergarten	*pupil*	*homework*
university	*student*	*notes*

Exercise 3
1) c, a, b   2) c, b, a   3) b, a, c   4) b, c, a   5) a, b, c

Just for fun
There are various possible answers to this exercise.

Unit 3.7

Exercise 1
1) b   2) d   3) a   4) c

Exercise 2
1) c   2) g   3) b   4) f   5) d   6) a   7) e

Exercise 3
1) e   2) d   3) c   4) f   5) a   6) b

Just for fun
There are various possible answers to this exercise.

Unit 3.8

Exercise 1
More than one answer is possible, but these are the suggested answers.
1) How old is Mullins?
2) When did the trial begin?
3) How did Mullins kill his wife?
4) Who gave evidence at the trial?
5) How long will Mullins have to stay in prison?
6) When will Mullins be released from prison?

Exercise 2
1) d   2) a   3) b   4) c

Exercise 3
1) e   2) b   3) f   4) i   5) j   6) k   7) c   8) a   9) h   10) d   11) g

Dictionary work
1) e   2) h   3) g   4) f   5) d   6) a   7) b   8) c

Unit 3.9

Exercise 1

1) a   2) b   3) c   4) c

Exercise 2

1) d   2) f   3) e   4) a   5) c   6) h   7) b   8) g

Exercise 3

1 (N) politics
2 (V) vote
3. (V) govern   4 (N) government
5 (V) elect   6 (A) presidential 7 (N) election
8 (N) politician   9 (A) political

Dictionary work

1) republic   2) political   3) industrial   4) president   5) politician   6) society
7) conservative   8) democracy   9) social   10) ambassador   11) democratic
12) economy   13) politics   14) industry   15) economic

Unit 3.10

Exercise 1

1) F   2) T   3) F   4) T   5) T   6) F   7) F

Exercise 2

1) astronaut   2) be launched   3) orbit

Exercise 3

1) b   2) h   3) e   4) d   5) g   6) f   7) a   8) c

Just for fun

1) e   2) c   3) a   4) f   5) b   6) d   7) g   8) i   9) h

Test yourself 6

1) astronaut   2) failed   3) voted   4) planet   5) temperature   6) headache
7) prison   8) kidnapping   9) shuttle   10) college   11) moon   12) princesses
13) homework   14) cough   15) witness   16) democracy   17) economic   18) pain
19) undergraduates   20) hurt/ache   21) arrested   22) satellites   23) take
24) government   25) trial